DAN-21   DANTES SUBJECT STANDARDIZED TESTS (DSST)

This is your
PASSBOOK for...

Introduction to Business

Test Preparation Study Guide
Questions & Answers

COPYRIGHT NOTICE

This book is SOLELY intended for, is sold ONLY to, and its use is RESTRICTED to individual, bona fide applicants or candidates who qualify by virtue of having seriously filed applications for appropriate license, certificate, professional and/or promotional advancement, higher school matriculation, scholarship, or other legitimate requirements of education and/or governmental authorities.

This book is NOT intended for use, class instruction, tutoring, training, duplication, copying, reprinting, excerption, or adaptation, etc., by:

1) Other publishers
2) Proprietors and/or Instructors of "Coaching" and/or Preparatory Courses
3) Personnel and/or Training Divisions of commercial, industrial, and governmental organizations
4) Schools, colleges, or universities and/or their departments and staffs, including teachers and other personnel
5) Testing Agencies or Bureaus
6) Study groups which seek by the purchase of a single volume to copy and/or duplicate and/or adapt this material for use by the group as a whole without having purchased individual volumes for each of the members of the group
7) Et al.

Such persons would be in violation of appropriate Federal and State statutes.

PROVISION OF LICENSING AGREEMENTS – Recognized educational, commercial, industrial, and governmental institutions and organizations, and others legitimately engaged in educational pursuits, including training, testing, and measurement activities, may address request for a licensing agreement to the copyright owners, who will determine whether, and under what conditions, including fees and charges, the materials in this book may be used them. In other words, a licensing facility exists for the legitimate use of the material in this book on other than an individual basis. However, it is asseverated and affirmed here that the material in this book CANNOT be used without the receipt of the express permission of such a licensing agreement from the Publishers. Inquiries re licensing should be addressed to the company, attention rights and permissions department.

All rights reserved, including the right of reproduction in whole or in part, in any form or by any means, electronic or mechanical, including photocopying, recording, or by any information storage and retrieval system, without permission in writing from the Publisher.

Copyright © 2025 by
National Learning Corporation

212 Michael Drive, Syosset, NY 11791
(516) 921-8888 • www.passbooks.com
E-mail: info@passbooks.com

PASSBOOK® SERIES

THE *PASSBOOK® SERIES* has been created to prepare applicants and candidates for the ultimate academic battlefield – the examination room.

At some time in our lives, each and every one of us may be required to take an examination – for validation, matriculation, admission, qualification, registration, certification, or licensure.

Based on the assumption that every applicant or candidate has met the basic formal educational standards, has taken the required number of courses, and read the necessary texts, the *PASSBOOK® SERIES* furnishes the one special preparation which may assure passing with confidence, instead of failing with insecurity. Examination questions – together with answers – are furnished as the basic vehicle for study so that the mysteries of the examination and its compounding difficulties may be eliminated or diminished by a sure method.

This book is meant to help you pass your examination provided that you qualify and are serious in your objective.

The entire field is reviewed through the huge store of content information which is succinctly presented through a provocative and challenging approach – the question-and-answer method.

A climate of success is established by furnishing the correct answers at the end of each test.

You soon learn to recognize types of questions, forms of questions, and patterns of questioning. You may even begin to anticipate expected outcomes.

You perceive that many questions are repeated or adapted so that you can gain acute insights, which may enable you to score many sure points.

You learn how to confront new questions, or types of questions, and to attack them confidently and work out the correct answers.

You note objectives and emphases, and recognize pitfalls and dangers, so that you may make positive educational adjustments.

Moreover, you are kept fully informed in relation to new concepts, methods, practices, and directions in the field.

You discover that you are actually taking the examination all the time: you are preparing for the examination by "taking" an examination, not by reading extraneous and/or supererogatory textbooks.

In short, this PASSBOOK®, used directedly, should be an important factor in helping you to pass your test.

NONTRADITIONAL EDUCATION

Students returning to school as adults bring more varied experience to their studies than do the teenagers who begin college shortly after graduating from high school. As a result, there are numerous programs for students with nontraditional learning curves. Hundreds of colleges and universities grant degrees to people who cannot attend classes at a regular campus or have already learned what the college is supposed to teach.

You can earn nontraditional education credits in many ways:
- Passing standardized exams
- Demonstrating knowledge gained through experience
- Completing campus-based coursework, and
- Taking courses off campus

Some methods of assessing learning for credit are objective, such as standardized tests. Others are more subjective, such as a review of life experiences.

With some help from four hypothetical characters – Alice, Vin, Lynette, and Jorge – this article describes nontraditional ways of earning educational credit. It begins by describing programs in which you can earn a high school diploma without spending 4 years in a classroom. The college picture is more complicated, so it is presented in two parts: one on gaining credit for what you know through course work or experience, and a second on college degree programs. The final section lists resources for locating more information.

Earning High School Credit

People who were prevented from finishing high school as teenagers have several options if they want to do so as adults. Some major cities have back-to-school programs that allow adults to attend high school classes with current students. But the more practical alternatives for most adults are to take the General Educational Development (GED) tests or to earn a high school diploma by demonstrating their skills or taking correspondence classes.

Of course, these options do not match the experience of staying in high school and graduating with one's friends. But they are viable alternatives for adult learners committed to meeting and, often, continuing their educational goals.

GED Program

Alice quit high school her sophomore year and took a job to help support herself, her younger brother, and their newly widowed mother. Now an adult, she wants to earn her high school diploma – and then go on to college. Because her job as head cook and her family responsibilities keep her busy during the day, she plans to get a high school equivalency diploma. She will study for, and take, the GED tests. Every year, about half a million adults earn their high school credentials this way. A GED diploma is accepted in lieu of a high school one by more than 90 percent of employers, colleges, and universities, so it is a good choice for someone like Alice.

The GED testing program is sponsored by the American Council on Education and State and local education departments. It consists of examinations in five subject areas: Writing, science, mathematics, social studies, and literature and the arts. The tests also measure skills such as analytical ability, problem solving, reading comprehension, and ability to understand and apply information. Most of the questions are multiple choice; the writing test includes an essay section on a topic of general interest.

Eligibility rules for taking the exams vary, but some states require that you must be at least 18. Tests are given in English, Spanish, and French. In addition to standard print, versions in large print, Braille, and audiocassette are also available. Total time allotted for the tests is 7 1/2 hours.

The GED tests are not easy. About one-fourth of those who complete the exams every year do not pass. Passing scores are established by administering the tests to a sample of graduating high school seniors. The minimum standard score is set so that about one-third of graduating seniors would not pass the tests if they took them.

Because of the difficulty of the tests, people need to prepare themselves to take them. Often, they start by taking the Official GED Practice Tests, usually available through a local adult education center. Centers are listed in your phone book's blue pages under "Adult Education," "Continuing Education," or "GED." Adult education centers also have information about GED preparation classes and self-study materials. Classes are generally arranged to accommodate adults' work schedules. National Learning Corporation publishes several study guides that aim to thoroughly prepare test-takers for the GED.

School districts, colleges, adult education centers, and community organizations have information about GED testing schedules and practice tests. For more information, contact them, your nearest GED testing center, or:

GED Testing Service
One Dupont Circle, NW, Suite 250
Washington, DC 20036-1163
1(800) 62-MY GED (626-9433)
(202) 939-9490

Skills Demonstration

Adults who have acquired high school level skills through experience might be eligible for the National External Diploma Program. This alternative to the GED does not involve any direct instruction. Instead, adults seeking a high school diploma must demonstrate mastery of 65 competencies in 8 general areas: Communication; computation; occupational preparedness; and self, social, consumer, scientific, and technological awareness.

Mastery is shown through the completion of the tasks. For example, a participant could prove competency in computation by measuring a room for carpeting, figuring out the amount of carpet needed, and computing the cost.

Before being accepted for the program, adults undergo an evaluation. Tests taken at one of the program's offices measure reading, writing, and mathematics abilities. A take-home segment includes a self-assessment of current skills, an individual skill evaluation, and an occupational interest and aptitude test.

Adults accepted for the program have weekly meetings with an assessor. At the meeting, the assessor reviews the participant's work from the previous week. If the task has not been completed properly, the assessor explains the mistake. Participants continue to correct their errors until they master each competency. A high school diploma is awarded upon proven mastery of all 65 competencies.

Fourteen States and the District of Columbia now offer the External Diploma Program. For more information, contact:

External Diploma Program
One Dupont Circle, NW, Suite 250
Washington, DC 20036-1193
(202) 939-9475

Correspondence and Distance Study
Vin dropped out of high school during his junior year because his family's frequent moves made it difficult for him to continue his studies. He promised himself at the time he dropped out that he would someday finish the courses needed for his diploma. For people like Vin, who prefer to earn a traditional diploma in a nontraditional way, there are about a dozen accredited courses of study for earning a high school diploma by correspondence, or distance study. The programs are either privately run, affiliated with a university, or administered by a State education department.

Distance study diploma programs have no residency requirements, allowing students to continue their studies from almost any location. Depending on the course of study, students need not be enrolled full time and usually have more flexible schedules for finishing their work. Selection of courses ranges from vo-tech to college prep, and some programs place different emphasis on the types of diplomas offered. University affiliated schools, for example, allow qualified students to take college courses along with their high school ones. Students can then apply the college credits toward a degree at that university or transfer them to another institution.

Taking courses by distance study is often more challenging and time consuming than attending classes, especially for adults who have other obligations. Success depends on each student's motivation. Students usually do reading assignments on their own. Written exercises, which they complete and send to an instructor for grading, supplement their reading material.

A list of some accredited high schools that offer diplomas by distance study is available free from the Distance Education and Training Council, formerly known as the National Home Study Council. Request the "DETC Directory of Accredited Institutions" from:

The Distance Education and Training Council
1601 18th Street, NW.
Washington, DC 20009-2529
(202) 234-5100

Some publications profiling nontraditional college programs include addresses and descriptions of several high school correspondence ones. See the Resources section at the end of this article for more information.

Getting College Credit For What You Know
Adults can receive college credit for prior coursework, by passing examinations, and documenting experiential learning. With help from a college advisor, nontraditional students should assess their skills, establish their educational goals, and determine the number of college credits they might be eligible for.

Even before you meet with a college advisor, you should collect all your school and training records. Then, make a list of all knowledge and abilities acquired through experience, no matter how irrelevant they seem to your chosen field. Next, determine your educational goals: What specific field do you wish to study? What kind of a degree do you want? Finally, determine how your past work fits into the field of study. Later on, you will evaluate educational programs to find one that's right for you.

People who have complex educational or experiential learning histories might want to have their learning evaluated by the Regents Credit Bank. The Credit Bank, operated by Regents College of the University of the State of New York, allows people to consolidate credits earned through college, experience, or other methods. Special assessments are available for Regents College enrollees whose knowledge in a specific field cannot be adequately evaluated by standardized exams. For more information, contact the Regents Credit Bank at:

Regents College
7 Columbia Circle
Albany, NY 12203-5159
(518) 464-8500

Credit For Prior College Coursework

When Lynette was in college during the 1970s, she attended several different schools and took a variety of courses. She did well in some classes and poorly in others. Now that she is a successful business owner and has more focus, Lynette thinks she should forget about her previous coursework and start from scratch. Instead, she should start from where she is.

Lynette should have all her transcripts sent to the colleges or universities of her choice and let an admissions officer determine which classes are applicable toward a degree. A few credits here and there may not seem like much, but they add up. Even if the subjects do not seem relevant to any major, they might be counted as elective credits toward a degree. And comparing the cost of transcripts with the cost of college courses, it makes sense to spend a few dollars per transcript for a chance to save hundreds, and perhaps thousands, of dollars in books and tuition.

Rules for transferring credits apply to all prior coursework at accredited colleges and universities, whether done on campus or off. Courses completed off campus, often called extended learning, include those available to students through independent study and correspondence. Many schools have extended learning programs; Brigham Young University, for example, offers more than 300 courses through its Department of Independent Study. One type of extended learning is distance learning, a form of correspondence study by technological means such as television, video and audio, CD-ROM, electronic mail, and computer tutorials. See the Resources section at the end of this article for more information about publications available from the National University Continuing Education Association.

Any previously earned college credits should be considered for transfer, no matter what the subject or the grade received. Many schools do not accept the transfer of courses graded below a C or ones taken more than a designated number of years ago. Some colleges and universities also have limits on the number of credits that can be transferred and applied toward a degree. But not all do. For example, Thomas Edison State College, New Jersey's State college for adults, accepts the transfer of all 120 hours of credit required for a baccalaureate degree – provided all the credits are transferred from regionally accredited schools, no more than 80 are at the junior college level, and the student's grades overall and in the field of study average out to C.

To assign credit for prior coursework, most schools require original transcripts. This means you must complete a form or send a written, signed request to have your transcripts released directly to a college or university. Once you have chosen the schools you want to apply to, contact the schools you attended before. Find out how much each transcript costs, and ask them to send your transcripts to the ones you are applying to. Write a letter that includes your name (and names used during attendance, if different) and dates of attendance, along with the names and addresses of the schools to which your transcripts should be sent. Include payment and mail to the registrar at the schools you have attended. The registrar's office will process your request and send an official transcript of your coursework to the colleges or universities you have designated.

Credit For Noncollege Courses

Colleges and universities are not the only ones that offer classes. Volunteer organizations and employers often provide formal training worth college credit. The American Council on Education has two programs that assess thousands of specific courses and make recommendations on the amount of college credit they are worth. Colleges and universities accept the recommendations or use them as guidelines.

One program evaluates educational courses sponsored by government agencies, business and industry, labor unions, and professional and voluntary organizations. It is the Program on Noncollegiate Sponsored Instruction (PONSI). Some of the training seminars Alice has participated in covered topics such as food preparation, kitchen safety, and nutrition. Although she has not yet earned her GED, Alice can earn college credit because of her completion of these formal job-training seminars. The number of credits each seminar is worth does not hinge on Alice's current eligibility for college enrollment.

The other program evaluates courses offered by the Army, Navy, Air Force, Marines, Coast Guard, and Department of Defense. It is the Military Evaluations Program. Jorge has never attended college, but the engineering technology classes he completed as part of his military training are worth college credit. And as an Army veteran, Jorge is eligible for a service that takes the evaluations one step further. The Army/American Council on Education Registry Transcript System (AARTS) will provide Jorge with an individualized transcript of American Council on Education credit recommendations for all courses he completed, the military occupational specialties (MOS's) he held, and examinations he passed while in the Army. All Army and National Guard enlisted personnel and veterans who enlisted after October 1981 are eligible for the transcript. Similar services are being considered by the Navy and Marine Corps.

To obtain a free transcript, see your Army Education Center for a 5454R transcript request form. Include your name, Social Security number, basic active service date, and complete address where you want the transcript sent. Mail your request to:
AARTS Operations Center
415 McPherson Ave.
Fort Leavenworth, KS 66027-1373

Recommendations for PONSI are published in *The National Guide to Educational Credit for Training Programs;* military program recommendations are in *The Guide to the Evaluation of Educational Experiences in the Armed Forces.* See the Resources section at the end of this article for more information about these publications.

Former military personnel who took a foreign language course through the Defense Language Institute may request course transcripts by sending their name, Social Security number, course title, duration of the course, and graduation date to:

> Commandant, Defense Language Institute
> Attn: ATFL-DAA-AR
> Transcripts
> Presidio of Monterey
> Monterey, CA 93944-5006

Not all of Jorge's and Alice's courses have been assessed by the American Council on Education. Training courses that have no Council credit recommendation should still be assessed by an advisor at the schools they want to attend. Course descriptions, class notes, test scores, and other documentation may be helpful for comparing training courses to their college equivalents. An oral examination or other demonstration of competency might also be required.

There is no guarantee you will receive all the credits you are seeking – but you certainly won't if you make no attempt.

Credit By Examination

Standardized tests are the best-known method of receiving college credit without taking courses. These exams are often taken by high school students seeking advanced placement for college, but they are also available to adult learners. Testing programs and colleges and universities offer exams in a number of subjects. Two U.S. Government institutes have foreign language exams for employees that also may be worth college credit.

It is important to understand that receiving a passing score on these exams does not mean you get college credit automatically. Each school determines which test results it will accept, minimum scores required, how scores are converted for credit, and the amount of credit, if any, to be assigned. Most colleges and universities accept the American Council on Education credit recommendations, published every other year in the 250-page *Guide to Educational Credit by Examination*. For more information, contact:

> The American Council on Education
> Credit by Examination Program
> One Dupont Circle, Suite 250
> Washington, DC 20036-1193
> (202) 939-9434

Testing programs:

You might know some of the five national testing programs by their acronyms or initials: CLEP, ACT PEP: RCE, DANTES, AP, and NOCTI. (The meanings of these initialisms are explained below.) There is some overlap among programs; for example, four of them have introductory accounting exams. Since you will not be awarded credit more than once for a specific subject, you should carefully evaluate each program for the subject exams you wish to take. And before taking an exam, make sure you will be awarded credit by the college or university you plan to attend.

CLEP (College-Level Examination Program), administered by the College Board, is the most widely accepted of the national testing programs; more than 2,800 accredited schools award credit for passing exam scores. Each test covers material taught in basic undergraduate courses. There are five general exams – English composition, humanities, college mathematics, natural sciences, and social sciences and history – and many subject exams. Most exams are entirely multiple-choice, but English composition exams may include an essay section. For more information, contact:

    CLEP
    P.O. Box 6600
    Princeton, NJ 08541-6600
    (609) 771-7865

ACT PEP: RCE (American College Testing Proficiency Exam Program: Regents College Examinations) tests are given in 38 subjects within arts and sciences, business, education, and nursing. Each exam is recommended for either lower- or upper-level credit. Exams contain either objective or extended response questions, and are graded according to a standard score, letter grade, or pass/fail. Fees vary, depending on the subject and type of exam. For more information or to request free study guides, contact:

    ACT PEP: Regents College Examinations
    P.O. Box 4014
    Iowa City, IA 52243
    (319) 337-1387
    (New York State residents must contact Regents College directly.)

DANTES (Defense Activity for Nontraditional Education Support) standardized tests are developed by the Educational Testing Service for the Department of Defense. Originally administered only to military personnel, the exams have been available to the public since 1983. About 50 subject tests cover business, mathematics, social science, physical science, humanities, foreign languages, and applied technology. Most of the tests consist entirely of multiple-choice questions. Schools determine their own administering fees and testing schedules. For more information or to request free study sheets, contact:

    DANTES Program Office
    Mail Stop 31-X
    Educational Testing Service
    Princeton, NJ 08541
    1(800) 257-9484

The AP (Advanced Placement) Program is a cooperative effort between secondary schools and colleges and universities. AP exams are developed each year by committees of college and high school faculty appointed by the College Board and assisted by consultants from the Educational Testing Service. Subjects include arts and languages, natural sciences, computer science, social sciences, history, and mathematics. Most tests are 2 or 3 hours long and include both multiple-choice and essay questions. AP courses are available to help students prepare for exams, which are offered in the spring. For more information about the Advanced Placement Program, contact:

    Advanced Placement Services
    P.O. Box 6671
    Princeton, NJ 08541-6671
    (609) 771-7300

NOCTI (National Occupational Competency Testing Institute) assessments are designed for people like Alice, who have vocational-technical skills that cannot be evaluated by other tests. NOCTI assesses competency at two levels: Student/job ready and teacher/experienced worker. Standardized evaluations are available for occupations such as auto-body repair, electronics, mechanical drafting, quantity food preparation, and upholstering. The tests consist of multiple-choice questions and a performance component. Other services include workshops, customized assessments, and pre-testing. For more information, contact:

NOCTI
500 N. Bronson Ave.
Ferris State University
Big Rapids, MI 49307
(616) 796-4699

Colleges and universities:

Many colleges and universities have credit-by-exam programs, through which students earn credit by passing a comprehensive exam for a course offered by the institution. Among the most widely recognized are the programs at Ohio University, the University of North Carolina, Thomas Edison State College, and New York University.

Ohio University offers about 150 examinations for credit. In addition, you may sometimes arrange to take special examinations in non-laboratory courses offered at Ohio University. To take a test for credit, you must enroll in the course. If you plan to transfer the credit earned, you also need written permission from an official at your school. Books and study materials are available, for a cost, through the university. Exams must be taken within 6 months of the enrollment date; most last 3 hours. You may arrange to take the exam off campus if you do not live near the university.

Ohio University is on the quarter-hour system; most courses are worth 4 quarter hours, the equivalent of 3 semester hours. For more information, contact:

Independent Study
Tupper Hall 302
Ohio University
Athens, OH 45701-2979
1(800) 444-2910
(614) 593-2910

The University of North Carolina offers a credit-by-examination option for 140 independent study (correspondence) courses in foreign languages, humanities, social sciences, mathematics, business administration, education, electrical and computer engineering, health administration, and natural sciences. To take an exam, you must request and receive approval from both the course instructor and the independent studies department. Exams must be taken within six months of enrollment, and you may register for no more than two at a time. If you are not near the University's Chapel Hill campus, you may take your exam under supervision at an accredited college, university, community college, or technical institute. For more information, contact:

Independent Studies
CB #1020, The Friday Center
UNC-Chapel Hill
Chapel Hill, NC 27599-1020
1(800) 862-5669 / (919) 962-1134

The Thomas Edison College Examination Program offers more than 50 exams in liberal arts, business, and professional areas. Thomas Edison State College administers tests twice a month in Trenton, New Jersey; however, students may arrange to take their tests with a proctor at any accredited American college or university or U.S. military base. Most of the tests are multiple choice; some also include short answer or essay questions. Time limits range from 90 minutes to 4 hours, depending on the exam. For more information, contact:

Thomas Edison State College
TECEP, Office of Testing and Assessment
101 W. State Street
Trenton, NJ 08608-1176
(609) 633-2844

New York University's Foreign Language Program offers proficiency exams in more than 40 languages, from Albanian to Yiddish. Two exams are available in each language: The 12-point test is equivalent to 4 undergraduate semesters, and the 16-point exam may lead to upper level credit. The tests are given at the university's Foreign Language Department throughout the year.

Proof of foreign language proficiency does not guarantee college credit. Some colleges and universities accept transcripts only for languages commonly taught, such as French and Spanish. Nontraditional programs are more likely than traditional ones to grant credit for proficiency in other languages.

For an informational brochure and registration form for NYU's foreign language proficiency exams, contact:

New York University
Foreign Language Department
48 Cooper Square, Room 107
New York, NY 10003
(212) 998-7030

Government institutes:

The Defense Language Institute and Foreign Service Institute administer foreign language proficiency exams for personnel stationed abroad. Usually, the tests are given at the end of intensive language courses or upon completion of service overseas. But some people – like Jorge, who knows Spanish – speak another language fluently and may be allowed to take a proficiency exam in that language before completing their tour of duty. Contact one of the offices listed below to obtain transcripts of those scores. Proof of proficiency does not guarantee college credit, however, as discussed above.

To request score reports from the Defense Language Institute for Defense Language Proficiency Tests, send your name, Social Security number, language for which you were tested, and, most importantly, when and where you took the exam to:

Commandant, Defense Language Institute
Attn: ATFL-ES-T
DLPT Score Report Request
Presidio of Monterey
Monterey, CA 93944-5006

To request transcripts of scores for Foreign Service Institute exams, send your name, Social Security number, language for which you were tested, and dates or year of exams to:

Foreign Service Institute
Arlington Hall
4020 Arlington Boulevard
Rosslyn, VA 22204-1500
Attn: Testing Office (Send your request to the attention of the testing office of the foreign language in which you were tested)

Credit For Experience

Experiential learning credit may be given for knowledge gained through job responsibilities, personal hobbies, volunteer opportunities, homemaking, and other experiences. Colleges and universities base credit awards on the knowledge you have attained, not for the experience alone. In addition, the knowledge must be college level; not just any learning will do. Throwing horseshoes as a hobby is not likely to be worth college credit. But if you've done research on how and where the sport originated, visited blacksmiths, organized tournaments, and written a column for a trade journal — well, that's a horseshoe of a different color.

Adults attempting to get credit for their experience should be forewarned: Having your experience evaluated for college credit is time-consuming, tedious work — not an easy shortcut for people who want quick-fix college credits. And not all experience, no matter how valuable, is the equivalent of college courses.

Requesting college credit for your experiential learning can be tricky. You should get assistance from a credit evaluations officer at the school you plan to attend, but you should also have a general idea of what your knowledge is worth. A common method for converting knowledge into credit is to use a college catalog. Find course titles and descriptions that match what you have learned through experience, and request the number of credits offered for those courses.

Once you know what credit to ask for, you must usually present your case in writing to officials at the college you plan to attend. The most common form of presenting experiential learning for credit is the portfolio. A portfolio is a written record of your knowledge along with a request for equivalent college credit. It includes an identification and description of the knowledge for which you are requesting credit, an explanatory essay of how the knowledge was gained and how it fits into your educational plans, documentation that you have acquired such knowledge, and a request for college credit. Required elements of a portfolio vary by schools but generally follow those guidelines.

In identifying knowledge you have gained, be specific about exactly what you have learned. For example, it is not enough for Lynette to say she runs a business. She must identify the knowledge she has gained from running it, such as personnel management, tax law, marketing strategy, and inventory review. She must also include brief descriptions about her knowledge of each to support her claims of having those skills.

The essay gives you a chance to relay something about who you are. It should address your educational goals, include relevant autobiographical details, and be well organized, neat, and convey confidence. In his essay, Jorge might first state his goal of becoming an engineer. Then he would explain why he joined the Army, where he got hands-on training and experience in developing and servicing electronic equipment.

This, he would say, led to his hobby of creating remote-controlled model cars, of which he has built 20. His conclusion would highlight his accomplishments and tie them to his desire to become an electronic engineer.

Documentation is evidence that you've learned what you claim to have learned. You can show proof of knowledge in a variety of ways, including audio or video recordings, letters from current or former employers describing your specific duties and job performance, blueprints, photographs or artwork, and transcripts of certifying exams for professional licenses and certification – such as Alice's certification from the American Culinary Federation. Although documentation can take many forms, written proof alone is not always enough. If it is impossible to document your knowledge in writing, find out if your experiential learning can be assessed through supplemental oral exams by a faculty expert.

Earning a College Degree

Nontraditional students often have work, family, and financial obligations that prevent them from quitting their jobs to attend school full time. Can they still meet their educational goals? Yes.

More than 150 accredited colleges and universities have nontraditional bachelor's degree programs that require students to spend little or no time on campus; over 300 others have nontraditional campus-based degree programs. Some of those schools, as well as most junior and community colleges, offer associate's degrees nontraditionally. Each school with a nontraditional course of study determines its own rules for awarding credit for prior coursework, exams, or experience, as discussed previously. Most have charges on top of tuition for providing these special services.

Several publications profile nontraditional degree programs; see the Resources section at the end of this article for more information. To determine which school best fits your academic profile and educational goals, first list your criteria. Then, evaluate nontraditional programs based on their accreditation, features, residency requirements, and expenses. Once you have chosen several schools to explore further, write to them for more information. Detailed explanations of school policies should help you decide which ones you want to apply to.

Get beyond the printed word – especially the glowing words each school writes about itself. Check out the schools you are considering with higher education authorities, alumni, employers, family members, and friends. If possible, visit the campus to talk to students and instructors and sit in on a few classes, even if you will be completing most or all of your work off campus. Ask school officials questions about such things as enrollment numbers, graduation rate, faculty qualifications, and confusing details about the application process or academic policies. After you have thoroughly investigated each prospective college or university, you can make an informed decision about which is right for you.

Accreditation

Accreditation is a process colleges and universities submit to voluntarily for getting their credentials. An accredited school has been investigated and visited by teams of observers and has periodic inspections by a private accrediting agency. The initial review can take two years or more.

Regional agencies accredit entire schools, and professional agencies accredit either specialized schools or departments within schools. Although there are no national accrediting standards, not just any accreditation will do. Countless "accreditation associations" have been invented by schools, many of which have no academic programs and sell phony degrees, to accredit themselves. But 6 regional and about 80 professional accrediting associations in the United States are recognized by the U.S. Department of Education or the Commission on Recognition of Postsecondary Accreditation. When checking accreditation, these are the names to look for. For more information about accreditation and accrediting agencies, contact:

>Institutional Participation Oversight Service Accreditation and State Liaison Division
>U.S. Department of Education
>ROB 3, Room 3915
>600 Independence Ave., SW
>Washington, DC 20202-5244
>(202) 708-7417

Because accreditation is not mandatory, lack of accreditation does not necessarily mean a school or program is bad. Some schools choose not to apply for accreditation, are in the process of applying, or have educational methods too unconventional for an accrediting association's standards. For the nontraditional student, however, earning a degree from a college or university with recognized accreditation is an especially important consideration. Although nontraditional education is becoming more widely accepted, it is not yet mainstream. Employers skeptical of a degree earned in a nontraditional manner are likely to be even less accepting of one from an unaccredited school.

Program Features

Because nontraditional students have diverse educational objectives, nontraditional schools are diverse in what they offer. Some programs are geared toward helping students organize their scattered educational credits to get a degree as quickly as possible. Others cater to those who may have specific credits or experience but need assistance in completing requirements. Whatever your educational profile, you should look for a program that works with you in obtaining your educational goals.

A few nontraditional programs have special admissions policies for adult learners like Alice, who plan to earn their GEDs but want to enroll in college in the meantime. Other features of nontraditional programs include individualized learning agreements, intensive academic counseling, cooperative learning and internship placement, and waiver of some prerequisites or other requirements – as well as college credit for prior coursework, examinations, and experiential learning, all discussed previously.

Lynette, whose primary goal is to finish her degree, wants to earn maximum credits for her business experience. She will look for programs that do not limit the number of credits awarded for equivalency exams and experiential learning. And since well-documented proof of knowledge is essential for earning experiential learning credits, Lynette should make sure the program she chooses provides assistance to students submitting a portfolio.

Jorge, on the other hand, has more credits than he needs in certain areas and is willing to forego some. To become an engineer, he must have a bachelor's degree; but because he is accustomed to hands-on learning, Jorge is interested in getting experience as he gains more technical skills. He will concentrate on finding schools with strong cooperative education, supervised fieldwork, or internship programs.

Residency Requirements

Programs are sometimes deemed nontraditional because of their residency requirements. Many people think of residency for colleges and universities in terms of tuition, with in-state students paying less than out-of-state ones. Residency also may refer to where a student lives, either on or off campus, while attending school.

But in nontraditional education, residency usually refers to how much time students must spend on campus, regardless of whether they attend classes there. In some nontraditional programs, students need not ever step foot on campus. Others require only a very short residency, such as one day or a few weeks. Many schools have standard residency requirements of several semesters but schedule classes for evenings or weekends to accommodate working adults.

Lynette, who previously took courses by independent study, prefers to earn credits by distance study. She will focus on schools that have no residency requirement. Several colleges and universities have nonresident degree completion programs for adults with some college credit. Under the direction of a faculty advisor, students devise a plan for earning their remaining credits. Methods for earning credits include independent study, distance learning, seminars, supervised fieldwork, and group study at arranged sites. Students may have to earn a certain number of credits through the degree-granting institution. But many programs allow students to take courses at accredited schools of their choice for transfer toward their degree.

Alice wants to attend lectures but has an unpredictable schedule. Her best course of action will be to seek out short residency programs that require students to attend seminars once or twice a semester. She can take courses that are televised and videotape them to watch when her schedule permits, with the seminars helping to ensure that she properly completes her coursework. Many colleges and universities with short residency requirements also permit students to earn some credits elsewhere, by whatever means the student chooses.

Some fields of study require classroom instruction. As Jorge will discover, few colleges and universities allow students to earn a bachelor's degree in engineering entirely through independent study. Nontraditional residency programs are designed to accommodate adults' daytime work schedules. Jorge should look for programs offering evening, weekend, summer, and accelerated courses.

Tuition and Other Expenses

The final decisions about which schools Alice, Jorge, and Lynette attend may hinge in large part on a single issue: Cost. And rising tuition is only part of the equation. Beginning with application fees and continuing through graduation fees, college expenses add up.

Traditional and nontraditional students have some expenses in common, such as the cost of books and other materials. Tuition might even be the same for some courses, especially for colleges and universities offering standard ones at unusual times. But for nontraditional programs, students may also pay fees for services such as credit or transcript review, evaluation, advisement, and portfolio assessment.

Students are also responsible for postage and handling or setup expenses for independent study courses, as well as for all examination and transcript fees for transferring credits. Usually, the more nontraditional the program, the more detailed the fees. Some schools charge a yearly enrollment fee rather than tuition for degree completion candidates who want their files to remain active.

Although tuition and fees might seem expensive, most educators tell you not to let money come between you and your educational goals. Talk to someone in the financial aid department of the school you plan to attend or check your library for publications about financial aid sources. The U.S. Department of Education publishes a guide to Federal aid programs such as Pell Grants, student loans, and work-study. To order the free 74-page booklet, *The Student Guide: Financial Aid from the U.S. Department of Education,* contact:

Federal Student Aid Information Center
P.O. Box 84
Washington, DC 20044
1 (800) 4FED-AID (433-3243)

Resources

Information on how to earn a high school diploma or college degree without following the usual routes is available from several organizations and in numerous publications. Information on nontraditional graduate degree programs, available for master's through doctoral level, though not discussed in this article, can usually be obtained from the same resources that detail bachelor's degree programs.

National Learning Corporation publishes study guides for all of these exams, for both general examinations and tests in specific subject areas. To order study guides, or to browse their catalog featuring more than 5,000 titles, visit NLC online at www.passbooks.com, or contact them by phone at (800) 632-8888.

Organizations

Adult learners should always contact their local school system, community college, or university to learn about programs that are readily available. The following national organizations can also supply information:

American Council on Education
One Dupont Circle
Washington, DC 20036-1193
(202) 939-9300

Within the American Council on Education, the Center for Adult Learning and Educational Credentials administers the National External Diploma Program, the GED Program, the Program on Noncollegiate Sponsored Instruction, the Credit by Examination Program, and the Military Evaluations Program.

DANTES Subject Standardized Tests

INTRODUCTION

The DANTES (Defense Activity for Non-Traditional Education Support) subject standardized tests are comprehensive college and graduate level examinations given by the Armed Forces, colleges and graduate schools as end-of-subject course evaluation final examinations or to obtain college equivalency credits in the various subject areas tested.

The DANTES Examination Program enables students to obtain college credit for what they have learned on the job, through self-study, personal interest, correspondence courses or by any other means. It is used by colleges and universities to award college credit to students who demonstrate that they know as much as students completing an equivalent college course. It is a cost-efficient, time-saving way for students to use their knowledge to accomplish their educational goals.

Most schools accept the American Council on Education (ACE) recommendations for the minimum score required and the amount of credit awarded, but not all schools do. Be sure to check the policy regarding the score level required for credit and the number of credits to be awarded.

Not all tests are accepted by all institutions. Even when a test is accepted by an institution, it may not be acceptable for every program at that institution. Before considering testing, ascertain the acceptability of a specific test for a particular course.

Colleges and universities that administer DANTES tests may administer them to any applicant – or they may administer the tests only to students registered at their institution. Decisions about who will be allowed to test are made by the school. Students should contact the test center to determine current policies and schedules for DANTES testing.

Colleges and universities authorized to administer DANTES tests usually do so throughout the calendar year. Each school sets its own fee for test administration and establishes its own testing schedule. Contact the representative at the administering school directly to make arrangements for testing.

Checklist For Students

- ✓ Visit **www.getcollegecredit.com** to obtain a list of tests, fact sheets, test preparation materials, participating colleges and universities, and much more.

- ✓ Contact your school advisor to confirm that the DSST you selected will fit into your curriculum.

- ✓ Consult the ***DSST Candidate Information Bulletin*** for answers to specific questions.

- ✓ Contact the test site to schedule your test.

- ✓ Prepare for your examination by using the fact sheet as a guide.

- ✓ Take the test.

If you would like a score report sent to your college or university, it is a good idea to bring the four-digit code with you. You must write the DSST Test Center Code for that institution on your answer sheet at the time of testing. DSST Test Center Codes are noted in the DSST Participating Colleges and Universities listing on the Web site.

If you prefer to send a score report to an institution at a later date, there is a transcript fee of $20 for each transcript ordered.

Thomson Prometric
DSST Program
2000 Lenox Drive, Third Floor
Lawrenceville, NJ 08648

Toll-free: 877-471-9860
609-895-5011

E-mail: pnj-dsst@thomson.com

MAKING A COLLEGE DEGREE WITHIN YOUR REACH

Today, there are many educational alternatives to the classroom—you can learn from your job, your reading, your independent study, and special interests you pursue. You may already have learned the subject matter covered by some college-level courses.

The DSST Program is a nationally recognized testing program that gives you the opportunity to receive college credit for learning acquired outside the traditional college classroom. Colleges and universities throughout the United States administer the program, developed by Thomson Prometric, year-round. Annually, over 90,000 DSSTs are administered to individuals who are interested in continuing their education. Take advantage of the DSST testing program; it speeds the educational process and provides the flexibility adults need, making earning a degree more feasible.

Since requirements differ from college to college, please check with the credit-awarding institution before taking a DSST. More than 1,800 colleges and universities currently award credit for DSSTs, and the number is growing every day. You can choose from 37 test titles in the areas of Social Science, Business, Mathematics, Applied Technology, Humanities, and Physical Science. A brief description of each examination is found on the pages that follow.

Reach Your Career Goals Through DSSTs

Use DSSTs to help you earn your degree, get a promotion, or simply demonstrate that you have college-level knowledge in subjects relevant to your work.

Save Time...

You don't have to sit through classes when you have previously acquired the knowledge or experience for most of what is being taught and can learn the rest yourself. You might be able to bypass introductory-level courses in subject areas you already know.

Save Money...

DSSTs save you money because the classes you bypass by earning credit through the DSST Program are classes you won't have to pay for on your way to earning your degree. You can use the money instead to take more advanced courses that can be more challenging and rewarding.

Improve Your Chances for Admission to College

Each college has its own admission policies; however, having passing scores for DSSTs on your transcript can provide strong evidence of how well you can perform at the college level.

Gain Confidence Performing at a College Level

Many adults returning to college find that lack of confidence is often the greatest hurdle to overcome. Passing a DSST demonstrates your ability to perform on a college level.

Make Up for Courses You May Have Missed

You may be ready to graduate from college and find that you are a few credits short of earning your degree. By using semester breaks, vacation time, or leisure time to study independently, you can prepare to take one or more DSSTs, fulfill your academic requirements, and graduate on time.

If You Cannot Attend Regularly Scheduled Classes...

If your lifestyle or responsibilities prevent you from attending regularly scheduled classes, you can earn your college degree from a college offering an external degree program. The DSST Program allows you to earn your degree by study and experience outside the traditional classroom.

Many colleges and universities offer external degree or distance learning programs. For additional information, contact the college you plan to attend or:

Center for Lifelong Learning
American Council on Education
One DuPont Circle NW, Suite 250
Washington, DC 20036
202-939-9475
www.acenet.edu
(Select "Center for Lifelong Learning" under "Programs & Services"
for more information)

Fact Sheets

For each test, there is a Fact Sheet that outlines the topics covered by each test and includes a list of sample questions, a list of recommended references of books that would be useful for review, and the number of credits awarded for a passing score as recommended by the American Council on Education (ACE). *Please note that some schools require scores that are higher than the minimum ACE-recommended passing score.* It is suggested that you check with your college or university to determine what score they require in order to earn credit. You can obtain Fact Sheets by:
- Downloading them from www.getcollegecredit.com
- E-mailing a request to pnj-dsst@thomson.com
- Completing a Candidate Publications Order Form

DSST Online Practice Tests

DSST online practice tests contain items that reflect a *partial range of difficulty* identified in the Content Outline section on each Fact Sheet. There is an online DSST Practice Test in the following categories:
- Mathematics
- Social Science
- Business
- Physical Science
- Applied Technology
- Humanities

Although the online DSST Practice Test questions do not indicate the full range of difficulty you would find in an actual DSST test, they will help you assess your knowledge level. Each online DSST Practice Test can be purchased by visiting www.getcollegecredit.com and clicking on DSST Practice Exams.

TAKING DSST EXAMINATIONS

Earning College Credit for DSST Examinations

To find out if the college of your choice awards credit for passing DSST scores, contact the admissions office or counseling and testing office. The college can also provide information on the scores required for awarding credit, the number of credit hours awarded, and any courses that can be bypassed with satisfactory scores.

It is important that you contact the institution of your choice as early as possible since credit-awarding policies differ among colleges and universities.

Where to Take DSSTs

DSSTs are administered at colleges and universities nationwide. Each location determines the frequency and scheduling of test administrations. To obtain the most current list of participating DSST colleges and universities:
- Visit and download the information from www.getcollegecredit.com
- E-mail pnj-dsst@thomson.com

Scheduling Your Examination

Please be aware that some colleges and universities provide DSST testing services to enrolled students only. After you have selected a college or university that administers DSSTs, you will need to contact them to schedule your test date.

The fee to take a DSST is $60 per test. This fee entitles you to two score reports after the test is scored. One will be sent directly to you and the other will be sent to the college or university that you designate on your answer sheet. You may pay the test fee with a certified check or U.S. money order made payable to Thomson Prometric or you may charge the test fee to your Visa, MasterCard or American Express credit card. Note: The credit card statement will reflect a charge from Thomson Prometric for all DSST examinations. *(Declined credit card charges will be assessed an additional $25 processing fee.)*

In addition, the test site may also require a test administration fee for each examination, to be paid directly to the institution. Contact the test site to determine its administration fee and payment policy.

Other Testing Arrangements

If you are unable to find a participating DSST college or university in your area, you may want to contact the testing office of a local accredited college or university to determine whether a representative from that office will agree to administer the test(s) for you.

The school's representative should then contact the DSST Program at 866-794-3497 to arrange for this administration. If you are unable to locate a test site, contact Thomson Prometric for assistance at pnj-dsst@thomson.com or 866-794-3497.

Testing Accommodations for Students with Disabilities

Thomson Prometric is committed to serving test takers with disabilities by providing services and reasonable testing accommodations as set forth in the provisions of the *Americans with Disabilities Act* (ADA). If you have a disability, as prescribed by the ADA, and require special testing services or arrangements, please contact the test administrator at the test site. You will be asked to submit to the test administrator documentation of your disability and your request for special accommodations. The test administrator will then forward your documentation along with your request for testing accommodations to Thomson Prometric for approval.

Please submit your request as far in advance of your test date as possible so that the necessary accommodations can be made. Only test takers with documented disabilities are eligible for special accommodations.

On the Day of the Examination

It is important to review this information and to have the correct identification present on the day of the examination:
- Arrive on time as a courtesy to the test administrator.
- Bring a valid form of government-issued identification that includes a current photo and your signature (acceptable documents include a driver's license, passport, state-issued identification card or military identification). *Anyone who fails to present valid identification will not be allowed to test.*
- Bring several No. 2 (soft-lead) sharpened pencils with good erasers, a watch, and a black pen if you will be writing an essay.
- Do not bring books or papers.
- Do not bring an alarm watch that beeps, a telephone, or a phone beeper into the testing room.
- The use of nonprogrammable calculators, slide rules, scratch paper and/or other materials is permitted for some of the tests.

DSST SCORING POLICIES

Your DSST examination scores are reported only to you, unless you request that they be sent elsewhere. If you want your scores sent to your college, you must provide the correct DSST code number of the school on your answer sheet at the time you take the test. See the *DSST Directory of Colleges and Universities* on the Web site www.getcollegecredit.com.

If your institution is not listed, contact Thomson Prometric at 866-794-3497 to establish a code number. (Some schools may require a student to be enrolled prior to receiving a score report.)

Receiving Your Score Report

Allow approximately four weeks after testing to receive your score report.

Calling DSST Customer Service before the required four-week score processing time has elapsed will not expedite the processing of your scores. Due to privacy and security requirements, scores will not be reported to students over the telephone under any circumstance.

Scoring of Principles of Public Speaking Speeches

The speech portion of the *Principles of Public Speaking* examination will be sent to speech raters who are faculty members at accredited colleges that currently teach or have previously taught the course. Scores for the *Principles of Public Speaking* examination are available six to eight weeks from receipt by Thomson Prometric. If you take the *Principles of Public Speaking* examination and fail (either the objective, speech portion, or both), you must follow the retesting policy waiting period of six months (180 days) before retaking the entire exam.

Essays

The essays for *Ethics in America* and *Technical Writing* are <u>optional</u> and thus are not scored by raters. The essays are forwarded to the college or university that you designate, along with your score report, for their use in determining the award of credit. <u>Before taking the *Ethics in America* or *Technical Writing* examinations, check with your college or university to determine whether the essay is required.</u>

NOTE: *Principles of Public Speaking* speech topic cassette tapes and essays are kept on file at Thomson Prometric for one year from the date of administration.

How to Get Transcripts

There is a $20 fee for each transcript you request. Payment must be in the form of a certified check, U.S. money order payable to Thomson Prometric, or credit card. Personal checks and debit cards are NOT an acceptable method of payment. One transcript may include scores for one or more examinations taken. To request a transcript, download the Transcript Order Form from www.getcollegecredit.com.

DESCRIPTION OF THE DSST EXAMINATIONS

Mathematics

- **Fundamentals of College Algebra** covers mathematical concepts such as fundamental algebraic operations; linear, absolute value; quadratic equations, inequalities, radials, exponents and logarithms, factoring polynomials and graphing. The use of a nonprogrammable, handheld calculator is permitted.

- **Principles of Statistics** tests the understanding of the various topics of statistics, both qualitatively and quantitatively, and the ability to apply statistical methods to solve a variety of problems. The topics included in this test are descriptive statistics; correlation and regression; probability; chance models and sampling and tests of significance. The use of a nonprogrammable, handheld calculator is permitted.

Social Science

- **Art of the Western World** deals with the history of art during the following periods: classical; Romanesque and Gothic; early Renaissance; high Renaissance, Baroque; rococo; neoclassicism and romanticism; realism, impressionism and post-impressionism; early twentieth century; and post-World War II.

- **Western Europe Since 1945** tests the knowledge of basic facts and terms and the understanding of concepts and principles related to the areas of the historical background of the aftermath of the Second World War and rebuilding of Europe; national political systems; issues and policies in Western European societies; European institutions and processes; and Europe's relations with the rest of the world.

- **An Introduction to the Modern Middle East** emphasizes core knowledge (including geography, Judaism, Christianity, Islam, ethnicity); nineteenth-century European impact; twentieth-century Western influences; World Wars I and II; new nations; social and cultural changes (1900-1960) and the Middle East from 1960 to present.

- **Human/Cultural Geography** includes the Earth and basic facts (coordinate systems, maps, physiography, atmosphere, soils and vegetation, water); culture and environment, spatial processes (social processes, modern economic systems, settlement patterns, political geography); and regional geography.

- **Rise and Fall of the Soviet Union** covers Russia under the Old Regime; the Revolutionary Period; New Economic Policy; Pre-war Stalinism; The Second World War; Post-war Stalinism; The Khrushchev Years; The Brezhnev Era; and reform and collapse.

- **A History of the Vietnam War** covers the history of the roots of the Vietnam War; the First Vietnam War (1946-1954); pre-war developments (1954-1963); American involvement in the Vietnam War; Tet (1968); Vietnamizing the War (1968-1973); Cambodia and Laos; peace; legacies and lessons.

- **The Civil War and Reconstruction** covers the Civil War from presecession (1861) through Reconstruction. It includes causes of the war; secession; Fort Sumter; the war in the east and in the west; major battles; the political situation; assassination of Lincoln; end of the Confederacy; and Reconstruction.

- **Foundations of Education** includes topics such as contemporary issues in education; past and current influences on education (philosophies, democratic ideals, social/economic influences); and the interrelationships between contemporary issues and influences.

- **Life-span Developmental Psychology** covers models and theories; methods of study; ethical issues; biological development; perception, learning and memory; cognition and language; social, emotional, and personality development; social behaviors, family life cycle, extrafamilial settings; singlehood and cohabitation; occupational development and retirement; adjustment to life stresses; and bereavement and loss.

- **Drug and Alcohol Abuse** includes such topics as drug use in society; classification of drugs; pharmacological principles; alcohol (types, effects of, alcoholism); general principles and use of sedative hypnotics, narcotic analgesics, stimulants, and hallucinogens; other drugs (inhalants, steroids); and prevention/treatment.

- **General Anthropology** deals with anthropology as a discipline; theoretical perspectives; physical anthropology; archaeology; social organization; economic organization; political organization; religion; and modernization and application of anthropology.

- **Introduction to Law Enforcement** includes topics such as history and professional movement of law enforcement; overview of the U.S. criminal justice system; police systems in the U.S.; police organization, management, and issues; and U.S. law and precedents.

- **Criminal Justice** deals with criminal behavior (crime in the U.S., theories of crime, types of crime); the criminal justice system (historical origins, legal foundations, due process); police; the court system (history and organization, adult court system, juvenile court, pre-trial and post-trial processes); and corrections.

- **Fundamentals of Counseling** covers historical development (significant influences and people); counselor roles and functions; the counseling relationship; and theoretical approaches to counseling.

Business
- **Principles of Finance** deals with financial statements and planning; time value of money; working capital management; valuation and characteristics; capital budgeting; cost of capital; risk and return; and international financial management. The use of a nonprogrammable, handheld calculator is permitted.

- **Principles of Financial Accounting** includes topics such as general concepts and principles, accounting cycle and classification; transaction analysis; accruals and deferrals; cash and internal control; current accounts; long- and short-term liabilities; capital stock; and financial statements. The use of a nonprogrammable, handheld calculator is permitted.

- **Human Resource Management** covers general employment issues; job analysis; training and development; performance appraisals; compensation issues; security issues; personnel legislation and regulation; labor relations and current issues; an overview of the Human Resource Management Field; Human Resource Planning; Staffing; training and development; compensation issues; safety and health; employee rights and discipline; employment law; labor relations and current issues and trends.

- **Organizational Behavior** deals with the study of organizational behavior (scientific approaches, research designs, data collection methods); individual processes and characteristics; interpersonal and group processes and characteristics; organizational processes and characteristics; and change and development processes.

- **Principles of Supervision** deals with the roles and responsibilities of the supervisor; management functions (planning, organization and staffing, directing at the supervisory level); and other topics (legal issues, stress management, union environments, quality concerns).

- **Business Law II** covers topics such as sales of goods; debtor and creditor relations; business organizations; property; and commercial paper.

- **Introduction to Computing** includes topics such as history and technological generations; hardware/software; applications to information technology; program development; data management; communications and connectivity; and computing and society. The use of a nonprogrammable, handheld calculator is permitted.

- **Management Information Systems** covers systems theory, analysis and design of systems, hardware and software; database management; telecommunications; management of the MIS functional area and informational support.

- **Introduction to Business** deals with economic issues affecting business; international business; government and business; forms of business ownership; small business, entrepreneurship and franchise; management process; human resource management; production and operations; marketing management; financial management; risk management and insurance; and management and information systems.

- **Money and Banking** covers the role and kinds of money; commercial banks and other financial intermediaries; central banking and the Federal Reserve system; money and macroeconomics activity; monetary policy in the U.S.; and the international monetary system.

- **Personal Finance** includes topics such as financial goals and values; budgeting; credit and debt; major purchases; taxes; insurance; investments; and retirement and estate planning. The use of auxiliary materials, such as calculators and slide rules, is NOT permitted.

- **Business Mathematics** deals with basic operations with integers, fractions, and decimals; round numbers; ratios; averages; business graphs; simple interest; compound interest and annuities; net pay and deductions; discounts and markups; depreciation and net worth; corporate securities; distribution of ownership; and stock and asset turnover.

Physical Science
• **Astronomy** covers the history of astronomy, celestial mechanics; celestial systems; astronomical instruments; the solar system; nature and evolution; the galaxy; the universe; determining astronomical distances; and life in the universe.

• **Here's to Your Health** covers mental health and behavior; human development and relationships; substance abuse; fitness and nutrition; risk factors, disease, and disease prevention; and safety, consumer awareness, and environmental concerns.

• **Environment and Humanity** deals with topics such as ecological concepts (ecosystems, global ecology, food chains and webs); environmental impacts; environmental management and conservation; and political processes and the future.

• **Principles of Physical Science I** includes physics: Newton's Laws of Motion; energy and momentum; thermodynamics; wave and optics; electricity and magnetism; chemistry: properties of matter; atomic theory and structure; and chemical reactions.

• **Physical Geology** covers Earth materials; igneous, sedimentary, and metamorphic rocks; surface processes (weathering, groundwater, glaciers, oceanic systems, deserts and winds, hydrologic cycle); internal Earth processes; and applications (mineral and energy resources, environmental geology).

Applied Technology
• **Technical Writing** covers topics such as theory and practice of technical writing; purpose, content, and organizational patterns of common types of technical documents; elements of various technical reports; and technical editing. Students have the option to write a short essay on one of the technical topics provided. Thomson Prometric will not score the essay; however, for determining the award of credit, a copy of the essay will be forwarded to the college or university you've designated along with the score report or transcript.

Humanities
• **Ethics in America** deals with ethical traditions (Greek views, Biblical traditions, moral law, consequential ethics, feminist ethics); ethical analysis of issues arising in interpersonal and personal-societal relationships and in professional and occupational roles; and relationships between ethical traditions and the ethical analysis of situations. Students have the option to write an essay to analyze a morally problematic situation in terms of issues relevant to a decision and arguments for alternative positions. Thomson Prometric will not score the essay; however, for determining the award of credit, a copy of the essay will be forwarded to the college or university you've designated along with the score report or transcript.

• **Introduction to World Religions** covers topics such as dimensions and approaches to religion; primal religions; Hinduism; Buddhism; Confucianism; Taoism; Judaism; Christianity; and Islam.

• **Principles of Public Speaking** consists of two parts: Part One consists of multiple-choice questions covering considerations of Principles of Public Speaking; audience analysis; purposes of speeches; structure/organization; content/supporting materials; research; language and style; delivery; communication apprehension; listening and feedback; and criticism and evaluation. Part Two requires the student to record an impromptu persuasive speech that will be scored.

FREQUENTLY ASKED QUESTIONS ABOUT DSSTs

In order to pass the test, must I study from one of the recommended references?

The recommended references are a listing of books that were being used as textbooks in college courses of the same or similar title at the time the test was developed. Appropriate textbooks for study are not limited to those listed in the fact sheet. If you wish to obtain study resources to prepare for the examination, you may reference either the current edition of the listed titles or textbooks currently used at a local college or university for the same class title. It is recommended that you reference more than one textbook on the topics outlined in the fact sheet. You should begin by checking textbook content against the content outline included on the front page of the DSST fact sheet before selecting textbooks that cover the text content from which to study. Textbooks may be found at the campus bookstore of a local college or university offering a course on the subject.

Is there a penalty for guessing on the tests?

There is no penalty for guessing on DSSTs, so you should mark an answer for each question.

How much time will I have to complete the test?

Many DSSTs can be completed within 90 minutes; however, additional time can be allowed if necessary.

What should I do if I find a test question irregularity?

Continue testing and then report the irregularity to the test administrator after the test. This may be done by asking that the test administrator note the irregularity on the Supervisor's Irregularity Report or you can write to Thomson Prometric, DSST Program, 2000 Lenox Drive, Third Floor, Lawrenceville, NJ 08648, and indicate the form and question number(s) or circumstances as well as your name and address.

When will I receive my score report?

Allow approximately four weeks from the date of testing to receive your score report. Allow six to eight weeks to receive a score report for the *Principles of Public Speaking* examination.

Will my test scores be released without my permission?

Your test score will not be released to anyone other than the school you designate on your answer sheet unless you write to us and ask us to send a transcript elsewhere. Instructions about how to do this can be found on your score report. Your scores may be used for research purposes, but individual scores are never made public nor are individuals identified if research findings are made public.

If I do not achieve a passing score on the test, how long must I wait until I can take the test again?

If you do not receive a score on the test that will enable you to obtain credit for the course, you may take the test again after six months (180 days). Please do not attempt to take the test before six months (180 days) have passed because you will receive a score report marked *invalid* and your test fee will not be refunded.

Can my test scores be canceled?

The test administrator is required to report any irregularities to Thomson Prometric. <u>The consequence of bringing unauthorized materials into the testing room, or giving or receiving help, will be the forfeiture of your test fee and the invalidation of test scores.</u> The DSST Program reserves the right to cancel scores and not issue score reports in such situations.

What can I do if I feel that my test scores were not accurately reported?

Thomson Prometric recognizes the extreme importance of test results to candidates and has a multi-step quality-control procedure to help ensure that reported scores are accurate. If you have reason to believe that your score(s) were not accurately reported, you may request to have your answer sheet reviewed and hand scored.

The fees for this service are:
- $20 fee if requested within six months of the test date
- $30 fee if requested more than six months from the test date
- $30 fee if a re-evaluation of the *Principles of Public Speaking* speech is requested

The fee for this service can be paid by credit card or by certified check or U.S. money order payable to Thomson Prometric. Submit your request for score verification along with the appropriate fee or credit card information (credit card number and expiration date) to Thomson Prometric, DSST Program, 2000 Lenox Drive, Third Floor, Lawrenceville, NJ 08648. Include your full name, the test title, the date you took the test, and your Social Security number. Candidates will be notified if a scoring discrepancy is discovered within four weeks of receipt of the request.

What does ACE recommendation mean?

The ACE recommendation is the minimum passing score recommended by the American Council on Education for any given test. It is equivalent to the average score of students in the DSST norming sample who received a grade of C for the course. Some schools require a score higher than the ACE recommendation.

Who is NLC?

National Learning Corporation (NLC) has been successfully preparing candidates for 40 years for over 5,000 exams. NLC publishes Passbook® study guides to help candidates prepare for all DANTES and CLEP exams and almost every other type of exam from high school through adult career.

Go to our website — www.passbooks.com — or call (800) 632-8888 for information about ordering our Passbooks.

To get detailed information on the DSST program and DSST preparation materials, visit www.getcollegecredit.com.

If you are interested in taking the DSST exams, call 877-471-9860 or e-mail pnj-dsst@thomson.com.

DANTES Subject Standardized Tests

INTRODUCTION TO BUSINESS

TEST INFORMATION

This test was developed to enable schools to award credit to students for knowledge equivalent to that which is learned by students taking the course. The school may choose to award college credit to the student based on the achievement of a passing score. The passing score for each examination is determined by the school based on recommendations from the American Council on Education (ACE). This minimum credit-awarding score is equal to the mean score of students in the norming sample who received a grade of C in the course. Some schools set their own standards for awarding credit and may require a higher score than the ACE recommendation. Students should obtain this information from the institution where they expect to receive credit.

CONTENT

The following topics, which are commonly taught in courses on this subject, are covered by this examination.

	Approximate Percent

I. Economic Issues Affecting Business
   A. Private enterprise
   B. Socialistic societies
   C. Today's business and its challenges
	14%

II. International Business	7%
III. Government and Business	5%
IV. Forms of Business Ownership	7%
V. Small Business, Entrepreneurship, and Franchise	5%

VI. Management Process
   A. Management functions and decision making
   B. Organizational strategies
   C. Human relations
   D. Business ethics, social responsibility, and the legal system
	12%

VII. Human Resource Management
   A. Human resource strategies
   B. Labor relations
	10%

VIII. Production and Operations	2%

IX. Marketing Management
   A. Marketing strategies
   B. Marketing mix
      1. Product
      2. Price
      3. Promotion
      4. Placement/distribution
	16%

X. Financial Management
   A. Money, banking, and financial institutions
   B. Financial strategies
   C. Securities market
	14%

XI. Risk Management and Insurance	3%

XII. Management and Information Systems
   A. Accounting
   B. Computers
	5%

from the official announcement for instructional purposes

Questions on the test require candidates to demonstrate the following abilities. Some questions may require more than one of the abilities.

- Knowledge of basic facts and terms (about 25-30% of the examination)

- Understanding of concepts and principles (about 30-35% of the examination)

- Ability to apply knowledge to specific case problems (about 35-40% of the examination)

SAMPLE QUESTIONS

1. Assets are defined as

    (A) everything a company owns
    (B) everything a company owes
    (C) a company's profits
    (D) the total of a company's equity capital

2. All of the following are necessary features of capitalism EXCEPT

    (A) profit
    (B) corporations
    (C) private ownership
    (D) competition

3. Business people who support involvement in social problems for humanitarian reasons usually believe that business

    (A) is responsible for most of society's problems
    (B) fulfills its social obligation by supplying jobs to millions of people
    (C) must follow the example of Andrew Carnegie
    (D) must put something back into the society from which it profits

4. All of the following are functions of management EXCEPT

    (A) controlling
    (B) selling
    (C) planning
    (D) organizing

5. Which of the following is a true statement about a job specification?

    (A) It describes the qualifications required of a worker.
    (B) It details the job's objectives.
    (C) It sets forth the relationship of the job to other jobs being performed within the firm.
    (D) It describes the working environment of the job.

6. All employees are required to join the union and pay dues in which of the following types of shop?

    (A) An open shop
    (B) A union shop
    (C) An agency shop
    (D) A closed shop

7. Since both drive up the cost of imported goods, there is little difference between import quotas and

    (A) embargoes
    (B) sanctions
    (C) tariffs
    (D) dumping

8. Which of the following are considered part of the marketing mix?

    I. Price
    II. Promotion
    III. Labor
    IV. Product

    (A) I and II only
    (B) III and IV only
    (C) I, II, and IV only
    (D) I, II, III, and IV

9. In order to cover risk, an insurance company must have a sufficient number of policyholders to do which of the following?

    (A) Examine the risk
    (B) Estimate probable loss
    (C) Construct actuarial tables
    (D) Average out the risk

10. Demand deposits are also know as

    (A) credit cards
    (B) charge accounts
    (C) savings accounts
    (D) checking accounts

11. The interest rate that banks charge their best corporate customers is the

    (A) prime rate
    (B) discount rate
    (C) credit rate
    (D) commercial rate

Correct Responses: 1.A; 2.B; 3.D; 4.B; 5.A; 6.B; 7.C; 8.C; 9.D; 10.D; 11.A

HOW TO TAKE A TEST

You have studied long, hard and conscientiously.

With your official admission card in hand, and your heart pounding, you have been admitted to the examination room.

You note that there are several hundred other applicants in the examination room waiting to take the same test.

They all appear to be equally well prepared.

You know that nothing but your best effort will suffice. The "moment of truth" is at hand: you now have to demonstrate objectively, in writing, your knowledge of content and your understanding of subject matter.

You are fighting the most important battle of your life—to pass and/or score high on an examination which will determine your career and provide the economic basis for your livelihood.

What extra, special things should you know and should you do in taking the examination?

I. YOU MUST PASS AN EXAMINATION

A. WHAT EVERY CANDIDATE SHOULD KNOW
Examination applicants often ask us for help in preparing for the written test. What can I study in advance? What kinds of questions will be asked? How will the test be given? How will the papers be graded?

B. HOW ARE EXAMS DEVELOPED?
Examinations are carefully written by trained technicians who are specialists in the field known as "psychological measurement," in consultation with recognized authorities in the field of work that the test will cover. These experts recommend the subject matter areas or skills to be tested; only those knowledges or skills important to your success on the job are included. The most reliable books and source materials available are used as references. Together, the experts and technicians judge the difficulty level of the questions.
Test technicians know how to phrase questions so that the problem is clearly stated. Their ethics do not permit "trick" or "catch" questions. Questions may have been tried out on sample groups, or subjected to statistical analysis, to determine their usefulness.
Written tests are often used in combination with performance tests, ratings of training and experience, and oral interviews. All of these measures combine to form the best-known means of finding the right person for the right job.

II. HOW TO PASS THE WRITTEN TEST

A. BASIC STEPS

1) Study the announcement

How, then, can you know what subjects to study? Our best answer is: "Learn as much as possible about the class of positions for which you've applied." The exam will test the knowledge, skills and abilities needed to do the work.

Your most valuable source of information about the position you want is the official exam announcement. This announcement lists the training and experience qualifications. Check these standards and apply only if you come reasonably close to meeting them. Many jurisdictions preview the written test in the exam announcement by including a section called "Knowledge and Abilities Required," "Scope of the Examination," or some similar heading. Here you will find out specifically what fields will be tested.

2) Choose appropriate study materials

If the position for which you are applying is technical or advanced, you will read more advanced, specialized material. If you are already familiar with the basic principles of your field, elementary textbooks would waste your time. Concentrate on advanced textbooks and technical periodicals. Think through the concepts and review difficult problems in your field.

These are all general sources. You can get more ideas on your own initiative, following these leads. For example, training manuals and publications of the government agency which employs workers in your field can be useful, particularly for technical and professional positions. A letter or visit to the government department involved may result in more specific study suggestions, and certainly will provide you with a more definite idea of the exact nature of the position you are seeking.

3) Study this book!

III. KINDS OF TESTS

Tests are used for purposes other than measuring knowledge and ability to perform specified duties. For some positions, it is equally important to test ability to make adjustments to new situations or to profit from training. In others, basic mental abilities not dependent on information are essential. Questions which test these things may not appear as pertinent to the duties of the position as those which test for knowledge and information. Yet they are often highly important parts of a fair examination. For very general questions, it is almost impossible to help you direct your study efforts. What we can do is to point out some of the more common of these general abilities needed in public service positions and describe some typical questions.

1) General information

Broad, general information has been found useful for predicting job success in some kinds of work. This is tested in a variety of ways, from vocabulary lists to questions about current events. Basic background in some field of work, such as sociology or economics, may be sampled in a group of questions. Often these are principles which have become familiar to most persons through exposure rather than through formal training. It is difficult to advise you how to study for these questions; being alert to the world around you is our best suggestion.

2) Verbal ability

An example of an ability needed in many positions is verbal or language ability. Verbal ability is, in brief, the ability to use and understand words. Vocabulary and grammar tests are typical measures of this ability. Reading comprehension or paragraph interpretation questions are common in many kinds of civil service tests. You are given a paragraph of written material and asked to find its central meaning.

IV. KINDS OF QUESTIONS

1. Multiple-choice Questions

Most popular of the short-answer questions is the "multiple choice" or "best answer" question. It can be used, for example, to test for factual knowledge, ability to solve problems or judgment in meeting situations found at work.

A multiple-choice question is normally one of three types:
- It can begin with an incomplete statement followed by several possible endings. You are to find the one ending which best completes the statement, although some of the others may not be entirely wrong.
- It can also be a complete statement in the form of a question which is answered by choosing one of the statements listed.
- It can be in the form of a problem – again you select the best answer.

Here is an example of a multiple-choice question with a discussion which should give you some clues as to the method for choosing the right answer:

When an employee has a complaint about his assignment, the action which will best help him overcome his difficulty is to
- A. discuss his difficulty with his coworkers
- B. take the problem to the head of the organization
- C. take the problem to the person who gave him the assignment
- D. say nothing to anyone about his complaint

In answering this question, you should study each of the choices to find which is best. Consider choice "A" – Certainly an employee may discuss his complaint with fellow employees, but no change or improvement can result, and the complaint remains unresolved. Choice "B" is a poor choice since the head of the organization probably does not know what assignment you have been given, and taking your problem to him is known as "going over the head" of the supervisor. The supervisor, or person who made the assignment, is the person who can clarify it or correct any injustice. Choice "C" is, therefore, correct. To say nothing, as in choice "D," is unwise. Supervisors have and interest in knowing the problems employees are facing, and the employee is seeking a solution to his problem.

2. True/False

3. Matching Questions

Matching an answer from a column of choices within another column.

V. RECORDING YOUR ANSWERS

Computer terminals are used more and more today for many different kinds of exams.

For an examination with very few applicants, you may be told to record your answers in the test booklet itself. Separate answer sheets are much more common. If this separate answer sheet is to be scored by machine – and this is often the case – it is highly important that you mark your answers correctly in order to get credit.

VI. BEFORE THE TEST

YOUR PHYSICAL CONDITION IS IMPORTANT

If you are not well, you can't do your best work on tests. If you are half asleep, you can't do your best either. Here are some tips:

1) Get about the same amount of sleep you usually get. Don't stay up all night before the test, either partying or worrying—DON'T DO IT!
2) If you wear glasses, be sure to wear them when you go to take the test. This goes for hearing aids, too.
3) If you have any physical problems that may keep you from doing your best, be sure to tell the person giving the test. If you are sick or in poor health, you relay cannot do your best on any test. You can always come back and take the test some other time.

Common sense will help you find procedures to follow to get ready for an examination. Too many of us, however, overlook these sensible measures. Indeed, nervousness and fatigue have been found to be the most serious reasons why applicants fail to do their best on civil service tests. Here is a list of reminders:

- Begin your preparation early – Don't wait until the last minute to go scurrying around for books and materials or to find out what the position is all about.
- Prepare continuously – An hour a night for a week is better than an all-night cram session. This has been definitely established. What is more, a night a week for a month will return better dividends than crowding your study into a shorter period of time.
- Locate the place of the exam – You have been sent a notice telling you when and where to report for the examination. If the location is in a different town or otherwise unfamiliar to you, it would be well to inquire the best route and learn something about the building.
- Relax the night before the test – Allow your mind to rest. Do not study at all that night. Plan some mild recreation or diversion; then go to bed early and get a good night's sleep.
- Get up early enough to make a leisurely trip to the place for the test – This way unforeseen events, traffic snarls, unfamiliar buildings, etc. will not upset you.
- Dress comfortably – A written test is not a fashion show. You will be known by number and not by name, so wear something comfortable.
- Leave excess paraphernalia at home – Shopping bags and odd bundles will get in your way. You need bring only the items mentioned in the official notice you received; usually everything you need is provided. Do not bring reference books to the exam. They will only confuse those last minutes and be taken away from you when in the test room.

- Arrive somewhat ahead of time – If because of transportation schedules you must get there very early, bring a newspaper or magazine to take your mind off yourself while waiting.
- Locate the examination room – When you have found the proper room, you will be directed to the seat or part of the room where you will sit. Sometimes you are given a sheet of instructions to read while you are waiting. Do not fill out any forms until you are told to do so; just read them and be prepared.
- Relax and prepare to listen to the instructions
- If you have any physical problem that may keep you from doing your best, be sure to tell the test administrator. If you are sick or in poor health, you really cannot do your best on the exam. You can come back and take the test some other time.

VII. AT THE TEST

The day of the test is here and you have the test booklet in your hand. The temptation to get going is very strong. Caution! There is more to success than knowing the right answers. You must know how to identify your papers and understand variations in the type of short-answer question used in this particular examination. Follow these suggestions for maximum results from your efforts:

1) Cooperate with the monitor

The test administrator has a duty to create a situation in which you can be as much at ease as possible. He will give instructions, tell you when to begin, check to see that you are marking your answer sheet correctly, and so on. He is not there to guard you, although he will see that your competitors do not take unfair advantage. He wants to help you do your best.

2) Listen to all instructions

Don't jump the gun! Wait until you understand all directions. In most civil service tests you get more time than you need to answer the questions. So don't be in a hurry. Read each word of instructions until you clearly understand the meaning. Study the examples, listen to all announcements and follow directions. Ask questions if you do not understand what to do.

3) Identify your papers

Civil service exams are usually identified by number only. You will be assigned a number; you must not put your name on your test papers. Be sure to copy your number correctly. Since more than one exam may be given, copy your exact examination title.

4) Plan your time

Unless you are told that a test is a "speed" or "rate of work" test, speed itself is usually not important. Time enough to answer all the questions will be provided, but this does not mean that you have all day. An overall time limit has been set. Divide the total time (in minutes) by the number of questions to determine the approximate time you have for each question.

5) Do not linger over difficult questions

If you come across a difficult question, mark it with a paper clip (useful to have along) and come back to it when you have been through the booklet. One caution if you do this – be sure to skip a number on your answer sheet as well. Check often to be sure that you have not lost your place and that you are marking in the row numbered the same as the question you are answering.

6) Read the questions

Be sure you know what the question asks! Many capable people are unsuccessful because they failed to read the questions correctly.

7) Answer all questions

Unless you have been instructed that a penalty will be deducted for incorrect answers, it is better to guess than to omit a question.

8) Speed tests

It is often better NOT to guess on speed tests. It has been found that on timed tests people are tempted to spend the last few seconds before time is called in marking answers at random – without even reading them – in the hope of picking up a few extra points. To discourage this practice, the instructions may warn you that your score will be "corrected" for guessing. That is, a penalty will be applied. The incorrect answers will be deducted from the correct ones, or some other penalty formula will be used.

9) Review your answers

If you finish before time is called, go back to the questions you guessed or omitted to give them further thought. Review other answers if you have time.

10) Return your test materials

If you are ready to leave before others have finished or time is called, take ALL your materials to the monitor and leave quietly. Never take any test material with you. The monitor can discover whose papers are not complete, and taking a test booklet may be grounds for disqualification.

VIII. EXAMINATION TECHNIQUES

1) Read the general instructions carefully. These are usually printed on the first page of the exam booklet. As a rule, these instructions refer to the timing of the examination; the fact that you should not start work until the signal and must stop work at a signal, etc. If there are any special instructions, such as a choice of questions to be answered, make sure that you note this instruction carefully.

2) When you are ready to start work on the examination, that is as soon as the signal has been given, read the instructions to each question booklet, underline any key words or phrases, such as least, best, outline, describe and the like. In this way you will tend to answer as requested rather than discover on reviewing your paper that you listed without describing, that you selected the worst choice rather than the best choice, etc.

3) If the examination is of the objective or multiple-choice type – that is, each question will also give a series of possible answers: A, B, C or D, and you are called upon to select the best answer and write the letter next to that answer on your answer paper – it is advisable to start answering each question in turn. There may be anywhere from 50 to 100 such questions in the three or four hours allotted and you can see how much time would be taken if you read through all the questions before beginning to answer any. Furthermore, if you

come across a question or group of questions which you know would be difficult to answer, it would undoubtedly affect your handling of all the other questions.

4) If the examination is of the essay type and contains but a few questions, it is a moot point as to whether you should read all the questions before starting to answer any one. Of course, if you are given a choice – say five out of seven and the like – then it is essential to read all the questions so you can eliminate the two that are most difficult. If, however, you are asked to answer all the questions, there may be danger in trying to answer the easiest one first because you may find that you will spend too much time on it. The best technique is to answer the first question, then proceed to the second, etc.

5) Time your answers. Before the exam begins, write down the time it started, then add the time allowed for the examination and write down the time it must be completed, then divide the time available somewhat as follows:
   - If 3-1/2 hours are allowed, that would be 210 minutes. If you have 80 objective-type questions, that would be an average of 2-1/2 minutes per question. Allow yourself no more than 2 minutes per question, or a total of 160 minutes, which will permit about 50 minutes to review.
   - If for the time allotment of 210 minutes there are 7 essay questions to answer, that would average about 30 minutes a question. Give yourself only 25 minutes per question so that you have about 35 minutes to review.

6) The most important instruction is to read each question and make sure you know what is wanted. The second most important instruction is to time yourself properly so that you answer every question. The third most important instruction is to answer every question. Guess if you have to but include something for each question. Remember that you will receive no credit for a blank and will probably receive some credit if you write something in answer to an essay question. If you guess a letter – say "B" for a multiple-choice question – you may have guessed right. If you leave a blank as an answer to a multiple-choice question, the examiners may respect your feelings but it will not add a point to your score. Some exams may penalize you for wrong answers, so in such cases only, you may not want to guess unless you have some basis for your answer.

7) Suggestions
   a. Objective-type questions
      1. Examine the question booklet for proper sequence of pages and questions
      2. Read all instructions carefully
      3. Skip any question which seems too difficult; return to it after all other questions have been answered
      4. Apportion your time properly; do not spend too much time on any single question or group of questions
      5. Note and underline key words – all, most, fewest, least, best, worst, same, opposite, etc.
      6. Pay particular attention to negatives
      7. Note unusual option, e.g., unduly long, short, complex, different or similar in content to the body of the question
      8. Observe the use of "hedging" words – probably, may, most likely, etc.

9. Make sure that your answer is put next to the same number as the question
10. Do not second-guess unless you have good reason to believe the second answer is definitely more correct
11. Cross out original answer if you decide another answer is more accurate; do not erase until you are ready to hand your paper in
12. Answer all questions; guess unless instructed otherwise
13. Leave time for review

b. Essay questions
1. Read each question carefully
2. Determine exactly what is wanted. Underline key words or phrases.
3. Decide on outline or paragraph answer
4. Include many different points and elements unless asked to develop any one or two points or elements
5. Show impartiality by giving pros and cons unless directed to select one side only
6. Make and write down any assumptions you find necessary to answer the questions
7. Watch your English, grammar, punctuation and choice of words
8. Time your answers; don't crowd material

8) Answering the essay question

Most essay questions can be answered by framing the specific response around several key words or ideas. Here are a few such key words or ideas:

M's: manpower, materials, methods, money, management
P's: purpose, program, policy, plan, procedure, practice, problems, pitfalls, personnel, public relations

a. Six basic steps in handling problems:
1. Preliminary plan and background development
2. Collect information, data and facts
3. Analyze and interpret information, data and facts
4. Analyze and develop solutions as well as make recommendations
5. Prepare report and sell recommendations
6. Install recommendations and follow up effectiveness

b. Pitfalls to avoid
1. Taking things for granted – A statement of the situation does not necessarily imply that each of the elements is necessarily true; for example, a complaint may be invalid and biased so that all that can be taken for granted is that a complaint has been registered
2. Considering only one side of a situation – Wherever possible, indicate several alternatives and then point out the reasons you selected the best one
3. Failing to indicate follow up – Whenever your answer indicates action on your part, make certain that you will take proper follow-up action to see how successful your recommendations, procedures or actions turn out to be
4. Taking too long in answering any single question – Remember to time your answers properly

EXAMINATION SECTION

EXAMINATION SECTION
TEST 1

DIRECTIONS: Each question or incomplete statement is followed by several suggested answers or completions. Select the one that BEST answers the question or completes the statement. *PRINT THE LETTER OF THE CORRECT ANSWER IN THE SPACE AT THE RIGHT.*

1. Which of the following is NOT a factor of production?

    A. Land
    B. Natural resources
    C. Promotion
    D. Capital

2. Country A has been growing wheat and corn for centuries to supply its own citizens. Country B also grows wheat and corn, but exports most of it. When Country A discovers huge amounts of crude oil beneath those fields previously used to grow corn and wheat, it must decide what to do.
Which of the following would give Country A comparative advantage?

    A. Devoting resources to extracting and exporting crude oil, and importing wheat and corn
    B. Continuing to grow its own wheat and corn
    C. Continuing to grow some wheat and corn, while exporting some oil
    D. Continuing to grow wheat and corn in order to export it

3. When a debtor can no longer meet financial obligations, he, she, or it must undergo this legal process in order to be relieved of those debts in order to start anew:

    A. breach of contract
    B. bankruptcy
    C. call provision
    D. criminal loss protection

4. The money left after a company distributes dividends to its stockholders is

    A. revenue
    B. profit
    C. net earnings
    D. retained earnings

5. The commercial law, adopted by every state, covering sales and commercial laws is called the

    A. Uniform Commercial Code
    B. Labor-Management Relations Act
    C. Federal Trade Commission Act
    D. General Agreement on Tariffs and Trade

6. A city, county, and/or state police force is an example of

    A. socialism
    B. public goods
    C. communism
    D. private goods

7. Funds raised within a company are considered

    A. debt capital
    B. revenue
    C. secured bonds
    D. equity capital

8. The StarDaze Lighting Company decides to order fewer glass orders with its glass supplier, due to a decline in sales. The glass supplier, in turn, lays off some of its workers, and those workers then have less money to spend on entertainment.
    This chain of events is known as

    A. the business cycle
    B. the multiplier effect
    C. recession
    D. supply-side economics

9. An economic system in which all or most of the means of production are privately owned and operated for profit is called

    A. capitalism
    B. communism
    C. democracy
    D. socialism

10. During a time of economic growth, if the government acts to adjust interest rates in order to dampen the economy, its actions are an example of

    A. disinflation
    B. financial sabotage
    C. monetary policy
    D. fiscal policy

11. The value of one currency in comparison to currencies of other countries is called the _____ rate.

    A. discount
    B. exchange
    C. market
    D. federal funds

12. Which of the following factors contribute to inflation?

    A. Government borrowing
    B. Increase in the price of imported goods
    C. Unemployment
    D. All of the above

13. Two consecutive quarters of negative growth in the real GNP is called

    A. stagflation
    B. inflation
    C. depression
    D. recession

14. The value of using a resource, measured against the best alternative to using that resource is called

    A. opportunity cost
    B. scarcity of resources
    C. innovation
    D. profit motive

15. Which of the following is considered capital?

    A. Labor
    B. Natural resources
    C. Buildings used to produce goods and services
    D. All of the above

16. What is a trial balance?

    A. Purchasing goods now and paying for them later
    B. A summary of all data in the ledgers in order to test the accuracy of the figures
    C. A line of credit temporarily guaranteed by a bank
    D. A loan payable in a period of over one year

17. Products used to produce other products are called

    A. industrial goods
    B. negotiable instruments
    C. tangible assets
    D. support goods

18. Bill Johnson is a United States importer trading in a time when the United States dollar is weak in comparison to foreign currencies. What will be the impact of this on Johnson and other United States importers?

    A. Importers will likely form a trade barrier.
    B. There will be no impact because demand for imports is not price sensitive.
    C. Import sales will increase.
    D. Import sales will decrease.

19. The distribution strategy which uses one retail outlet in a given geographic area is called _____ distribution.

    A. corporate
    B. contractual
    C. exclusive
    D. intensive

20. Susan Williams owns a florist shop. She must decide whether to spend $500 on seasonal flowers for the holiday season and cut back on regular stock. Her choice is an example of

    A. opportunity cost
    B. innovation
    C. scarcity of resources
    D. profit motive

21. A promissory note which requires the borrower to repay the loan in specified installments is called a

    A. trade deficit
    B. long-term loan
    C. term loan agreement
    D. trade credit

22. Selling accounts receivable for cash is called

    A. hedging
    B. inventory financing
    C. pledging
    D. factoring

23. An entrepreneur who invests money and effort into producing a product, and then brings it to the market is exhibiting

    A. the profit motive
    B. opportunity cost
    C. the charity motive
    D. the quality motive

24. When a bank issues a note which earns a guaranteed interest for a fixed period of time, it is called a

    A. bond
    B. convertible bond
    C. certificate of deposit
    D. debenture bond

25. Which of the following is a DISADVANTAGE of a sole proprietorship?

    A. Strict government reporting requirements
    B. Difficulty with forming them
    C. Difficulties among partners
    D. Unlimited liability

KEY (CORRECT ANSWERS)

1. C
2. A
3. B
4. D
5. A

6. B
7. D
8. B
9. A
10. D

11. B
12. D
13. D
14. A
15. C

16. B
17. A
18. D
19. C
20. A

21. C
22. D
23. A
24. C
25. D

TEST 2

DIRECTIONS: Each question or incomplete statement is followed by several suggested answers or completions. Select the one that BEST answers the question or completes the statement. *PRINT THE LETTER OF THE CORRECT ANSWER IN THE SPACE AT THE RIGHT.*

1. This type of unemployment results from people losing their jobs when their occupation is no longer part of the main structure of the economy. 1.____

    A. Structural
    B. Seasonal
    C. Frictional
    D. Cyclical

2. Which of the following is an example of an institutional investor? 2.____

    A. Individual investor in a mutual fund
    B. Voting stockholder
    C. Mutual fund
    D. Non-voting stockholder

3. When a manager acts as a resource allocator, what type of role is he/she fulfilling? 3.____

    A. Leadership
    B. Decision-making
    C. Informational
    D. Liaison

4. Which of the following steps are required for starting a partnership? 4.____
    I. Obtaining invoices and other business invoices
    II. Opening a checking account for business
    III. Creating a buy/sell agreement
    IV. Choosing a state in which to incorporate

    The CORRECT answer is:

    A. I, III, IV
    B. II, III, IV
    C. I, II, III
    D. I, II, III, IV

5. Which of the following is a middle-management position? 5.____

    A. CEO
    B. Supervisor
    C. Foreman
    D. Plant manager

6. The financial position of a firm at a specific date is reported on a(n) 6.____

    A. balance sheet
    B. bookkeeping ledger
    C. accounting report
    D. certificate of deposit

7. A consumer's right to be informed includes which of the following? 7.____

    A. The ability to be heard
    B. The ability to trust that a product is safe
    C. Knowing what is in a product
    D. The ability to choose between products

8. When employees, managers or investors attempt to purchase an organization through borrowing, it is called 8.____

    A. a leveraged buyout
    B. a hostile takeover
    C. a call provision
    D. buying on margin

9. Which of the following is an example of a product franchise?

   A. Coca-Cola bottling plant
   B. Car dealer
   C. Boston Chicken
   D. Shell gas station

10. The classical theory of motivation holds that _____ is the sole motivator in the workplace.

    A. fairness
    B. ethics
    C. success
    D. money

11. Government regulations limiting the import of goods and services in order to protect domestic producers is referred to as

    A. a primary boycott
    B. a protective tariff
    C. trade protectionism
    D. a closed-shop agreement

12. Which of the following is an employee-oriented motivational technique?

    A. Job sharing
    B. Flextime
    C. Job enrichment
    D. Behavior modification

13. This law forbids contracts, combinations or conspiracies in restraint of trade, monopolies or attempts to monopolize.

    A. Robinson-Patman Act
    B. Sherman Anti-Trust Act
    C. National Labor Relations Act
    D. General Agreement on Tariffs and Trade

14. The sale of part of a company is known as

    A. divestiture
    B. leveraged buyout
    C. merger
    D. hostile takeover

15. The law which prohibits any practice which will result in a monopoly is the

    A. Federal Trade Commission Act
    B. General Agreement on Tariffs and Trade
    C. Clayton Act
    D. Robinson-Patman Act

16. What is the most common fringe benefit provided by employers?

    A. Paid holidays
    B. Stock ownership
    C. Retirement benefits
    D. Insurance

17. _____ liability provides no legal defense for placing a product on the market that is dangerous to the consumer because of known or knowable defects.

    A. Unlimited
    B. Strict
    C. Limited
    D. Rule of indemnity

18. Trying to extend the life cycle of products by changing features of the product is called

    A. product differentiation
    B. market segmentation
    C. target marketing
    D. product modification

19. Which economic system grants the government the greatest degree of ownership and control?

    A. Socialism
    B. Capitalism
    C. Communism
    D. Modified capitalism

20. The distribution system which uses a preferred group of retailers in an area is called

    A. selective distribution
    B. spot marketing
    C. exclusive distribution
    D. the push strategy

21. Which of the following are among the most common forces of international business activity?
    I. Importing and exporting
    II. Tariffs and embargoes
    III. Licensing and franchising

    The CORRECT answer is:

    A. I, II
    B. I, III
    C. II, III
    D. I, II, III

22. An owner in a business who has no management responsibility or liability for losses beyond the original investment is a

    A. chief financial officer (CFO)
    B. general partner
    C. limited partner
    D. small business entrepreneur

23. An economy which combines free markets with government allocation of some resources is a(n)

    A. mixed economy
    B. oligopoly
    C. communist economy
    D. capitalist economy

24. A corporation whose stock is owned entirely (or almost entirely) by another corporation is called a

    A. private corporation
    B. professional corporation
    C. parent company
    D. subsidiary corporation

25. A country with a monopoly on producing a product (or a country able to produce a product at a cost below that of all other countries) has a(n)

    A. oligopoly
    B. absolute advantage
    C. penetration strategy advantage
    D. absolute liability

KEY (CORRECT ANSWERS)

1. A
2. C
3. B
4. C
5. D
6. A
7. C
8. A
9. B
10. D

11. C
12. D
13. B
14. A
15. C
16. D
17. B
18. D
19. C
20. A

21. B
22. C
23. A
24. D
25. B

EXAMINATION SECTION
TEST 1

DIRECTIONS: Each question or incomplete statement is followed by several suggested answers or completions. Select the one that BEST answers the question or completes the statement. *PRINT THE LETTER OF THE CORRECT ANSWER IN THE SPACE AT THE RIGHT.*

1. Compensation based on bonuses which are rewarded when employees meet specific goals is termed   1.____

   A. knowledge-based pay
   B. pay for performance
   C. profit-sharing
   D. goal-sharing

2. An unsecured bond is a _____ bond.   2.____

   A. debenture
   B. discount
   C. convertible
   D. surety

3. An entity which buys stocks and then sells shares to the public is called a   3.____

   A. brokerage firm
   B. commercial bank
   C. mutual fund
   D. credit union

4. Which subgroup describes a consumer market?   4.____

   A. A government market
   B. People who need or want products with the money to buy them
   C. A reseller market
   D. An industrial/commercial market

5. A chart or table made up of rows or columns, which allows a manager to organize information, is called a   5.____

   A. balance sheet
   B. business plan
   C. cash-flow forecast
   D. spreadsheet

6. The use of advertising and/or highly trained salespeople to inform customers about a product is an example of which aspect of the marketing mix?   6.____

   A. Promotion   B. Product   C. Price   D. Place

7. When members of an organization share values and traditions, they share a(n)   7.____

   A. open system
   B. organizational culture
   C. organizational design
   D. management-by-objectives system

8. The use of celebrities as endorsers for products is an example of which aspect of buyer behavior?   8.____

   A. Culture
   B. Reference groups
   C. Social class
   D. Self-image

9. When a person is granted sole rights to a book, he/she has received a

   A. patent
   B. franchise
   C. copyright
   D. contract

10. Pricing a product low in order to attract more customers and discourage competitors is

    A. demand-oriented pricing
    B. a penetration strategy
    C. a pull strategy
    D. competition-oriented pricing

11. Using promotional tools to motivate customers into requesting products from stores is called

    A. penetration strategy
    B. push strategy
    C. pull strategy
    D. selective distribution

12. The purpose of the index of leading economic indicators is to

    A. facilitate recovery from recession
    B. track changes in the stock market
    C. prevent recession
    D. predict changes in the business cycle

13. The relationship of exports to imports is called

    A. debt capital
    B. cash flow forecast
    C. balance of payments
    D. balance of merchandise trade

14. Instructions to a broker to buy stock at the best current price is called

    A. a limit order
    B. pledging
    C. a lender offer
    D. a market order

15. Which of the following situations describes an absolute advantage?
    Country A

    A. has superior technology in growing flowers which it exports, while importing other products
    B. uses its land resources to grow corn and wheat while importing crude oil
    C. has unlimited sources of cheap labor with which to produce handmade clothes for export
    D. has superior technology in electronics, but few land resources

16. Inflation caused by rising business costs is called

    A. cost-push inflation
    B. demand-pull inflation
    C. deflation
    D. stagflation

17. Deciding which ideas, goods and/or services will attract customers is part of which aspect of the marketing mix?

    A. Price   B. Place   C. Promotion   D. Product

18. Contracts which, as condition of employment, required employees to agree not to join unions were called

    A. agency-shop agreements
    B. yellow-dog contracts
    C. collective bargaining contracts
    D. lockouts

19. The strategy used to extend the life-cycle of products by finding new users is called

    A. market targeting
    B. dumping
    C. market modification
    D. market segmentation

20. Which of the following are the most common forms of business ownership?
    I. Corporation
    II. Franchise
    III. Partnership
    IV. Sole proprietorship

    The CORRECT answer is:

    A. I, II, III
    B. II, III, IV
    C. I, IV
    D. I, III, IV

21. The short-term equivalent of a corporate IOU which is sold by firm is called a(n)

    A. convertible bond
    B. discount bond
    C. income stock
    D. commercial paper

22. Sam the Hot Dog Man decided to lower prices for his hot dogs from $2.50 to $2.00 in order to attract more customers. His decision sparked a price war among the other convenience food restaurants in his area.
    This is an example of what element of competition?

    A. Innovation
    B. Quality
    C. Price
    D. All of the above

23. In the example in Question 22 above, how will Sam and the other businesses best maintain their profit margins with lowered prices?

    A. Increase efficiency
    B. Lower business costs
    C. Work to attract repeat customers
    D. All of the above

24. Which of the following are steps in the cycle of control?
    I. Set standards
    II. Measure performance
    III. Audit and observe
    IV. Compare performance to standards

    The CORRECT answer is:

    A. I, III, IV
    B. I, II, IV
    C. II, III, IV
    D. I, II, III

25. Individuals that invest in new businesses in exchange for partial ownership in the company are called   25._____

    A. venture capitalists
    B. investors
    C. stockholders
    D. entrepreneurs

KEY (CORRECT ANSWERS)

1. B
2. A
3. C
4. B
5. D

6. A
7. B
8. D
9. C
10. B

11. C
12. D
13. D
14. D
15. C

16. A
17. D
18. B
19. C
20. D

21. D
22. C
23. D
24. B
25. A

TEST 2

DIRECTIONS: Each question or incomplete statement is followed by several suggested answers or completions. Select the one that BEST answers the question or completes the statement. *PRINT THE LETTER OF THE CORRECT ANSWER IN THE SPACE AT THE RIGHT.*

1. When the market has many buyers and sellers, and no seller is large enough to determine the price of product, then we have

    A. a monopoly
    B. perfect competition
    C. an oligopoly
    D. a mixed economy

2. A bond that can be converted into shares of common stock is a

    A. convertible bond
    B. discount bond
    C. debenture bond
    D. certificate of deposit

3. When a company wants to serve a single market segment, it follows which approach to market segmentation?

    A. Differentiated
    B. Undifferentiated
    C. Concentrated
    D. Customized

4. A person who buys and sells securities for clients is a

    A. wholesaler
    B. retailer
    C. stockbroker
    D. marketing middleman

5. Income from legal business activities which is not reported to the government is part of the

    A. GNP
    B. underground economy
    C. GDP
    D. black market economy

6. Which of the following has nonprofit status?

    A. Credit unions
    B. National banks
    C. State banks
    D. All of the above

7. The _____ is the United Nations agency which borrows money from prosperous countries and lends it to less-prosperous countries at favorable rates.

    A. International Trade Commission
    B. Federal Reserve System
    C. World Bank
    D. International Monetary Fund (IMF)

8. When a company views each customer as a separate market segment, it is following the _____ approach to market segmentation.

    A. customized
    B. concentrated
    C. undifferentiated
    D. differentiated

9. The process of testing products among potential users is called

    A. trade advertising
    B. test marketing
    C. promotion
    D. publicity

13

10. A _____ is an example of an organizational market.

   A. furniture store specializing in home office and conventional furniture
   B. copy store where people can photocopy personal items
   C. stationery store where people can buy paper products for personal use
   D. copy machine company who sells machines to corporations

11. The Federal Reserve charges the _____ rate to other bank for loans.

   A. exchange
   B. discount
   C. federal funds
   D. market

12. Stock which gives owners an early claim on assets if a business is sold is called _____ stock.

   A. preferred
   B. cumulative preferred
   C. common
   D. blue-chip

13. Which of the following generally charges the highest rate of interest for a loan?

   A. Commercial bank
   B. Credit union
   C. Savings and loan
   D. Finance company

14. People who predict future losses based on the analysis of historical data are called

   A. accountants
   B. investors
   C. actuaries
   D. contingency planners

15. The percentage of depositors' money that banks must set aside in order to meet projected withdrawals is called the

   A. reserve requirement
   B. open-market operation
   C. selective credit control
   D. margin requirement

16. A demand curve provides the

   A. quantity of goods producers will provide at a particular date
   B. relationship between price and quantity demanded
   C. point at which quantity supplied and demanded are in balance
   D. relationship between price and quantity supplied

17. Which of the following is a characteristic of transactional leadership?

   A. Motivating employees to perform at expected levels
   B. Instilling confidence in employees' ability to go beyond their own expectations
   C. Inspiring employees to perform beyond their own self-interest
   D. Motivating employees to perform beyond expected levels

18. A proposal to purchase all or part of a firm's stock at a price above the current market value is called a

   A. merger
   B. stock split
   C. market segmentation
   D. tender offer

19. An unwelcome sexual advance in the workplace which negatively affects a woman's job prospects is an example of

    A. the glass ceiling
    B. sexual abuse
    C. sexual harassment
    D. discrimination

20. A form of fraud in which early investors are paid with money raised by later investors is called

    A. a ponzi scheme
    B. corporate raiding
    C. discrimination
    D. insider trading

21. Buying goods now in order to pay for them early and receive a discount is called a

    A. trade deficit
    B. trade credit
    C. secured loan
    D. secured bond

22. It is legal to ask a prospective employee in an interview

    A. whether he or she owns or rents a home
    B. whether he or she owes child support
    C. whether he or she belongs to a union
    D. why he/she wishes to change his/her job

23. The pricing strategy based on all other competitors' prices is called

    A. demand-oriented pricing
    B. competition-oriented pricing
    C. cost-push inflation
    D. long-term financing

24. The assumptions of Management Theory X correlates to which of the following management styles?

    A. Transformational
    B. Laissez-faire
    C. Authoritarian
    D. Participative

25. A contract of indebtedness which is issued by a corporation and promises payment of a principal amount at a specified future time plus interest is called a

    A. contract
    B. convertible bond
    C. demand deposit
    D. bond

KEY (CORRECT ANSWERS)

1.	B	11.	B
2.	A	12.	A
3.	C	13.	D
4.	C	14.	C
5.	B	15.	A
6.	A	16.	B
7.	C	17.	A
8.	A	18.	D
9.	B	19.	C
10.	D	20.	A

21. B
22. D
23. B
24. C
25. D

EXAMINATION SECTION
TEST 1

DIRECTIONS: Each question or incomplete statement is followed by several suggested answers or completions. Select the one that BEST answers the question or completes the statement. *PRINT THE LETTER OF THE CORRECT ANSWER IN THE SPACE AT THE RIGHT.*

1. The face amount of a bond is called   1._____

   A. principal
   C. equity
   B. par value
   D. market price

2. The point at which quantity supplied and quantity demanded are balanced is called the   2._____

   A. demand curve
   C. supply curve
   B. equilibrium price
   D. demand

3. Stagnant economic conditions combined with inflation is called   3._____

   A. inflation
   C. depression
   B. recession
   D. stagflation

4. Which of the following are forms of franchises?   4._____
   I. Product
   II. Service
   III. Manufacturing
   IV. Business format

   The CORRECT answer is:

   A. I, II, III
   C. I, III, IV
   B. II, III, IV
   D. I, II, IV

5. The statistic which measures changes in the price of goods and services bought by consumers is the   5._____

   A. international monetary fund
   B. NASDAQ
   C. stock exchange
   D. consumer price index

6. Using borrowed money to finance an investment is called   6._____

   A. leverage
   C. capital budgeting
   B. trade credit
   D. cost of capital

7. A spending plan for assets whose returns are expected to return over a period of more than one year is called a   7._____

   A. balance sheet
   C. cash flow forecast
   B. capital budget
   D. long-term forecast

8. Estimating the flow of funds into a business on a month-by-month basis is part of the   8._____

   A. leverage process
   B. capital budgeting process
   C. financial management process
   D. cost of capital

17

9. Economic resources owned by a firm are called

   A. benefits
   B. commodities
   C. liabilities
   D. assets

10. Money used to buy something of permanent value in a business is called

    A. capital investment
    B. leverage
    C. capital budgeting
    D. trade credit

11. The government agency that has responsibility for regulating the various exchanges is the

    A. Federal Deposit Insurance Corporation
    B. Securities and Exchange Commission
    C. Federal Trade Commission
    D. National Association of Securities Dealers Automated Quotation System (NASDAQ)

12. Junk, serial, debenture, and callable are all types of

    A. unsecured loans
    B. stocks
    C. leases
    D. bonds

13. The money available for purchasing nonessential items after taxes and essentials is termed

    A. net income
    B. assets
    C. discretionary income
    D. disposable income

14. Common, preferred, and authorized are all types of

    A. unsecured loans
    B. leases
    C. bonds
    D. stocks

15. Marketing middlemen who sell to organizations and individuals, but not to final customers, are called

    A. wholesalers
    B. brokers
    C. arbitrators
    D. drop shippers

16. Which of the following pays the highest interest because it is below investment grade?

    A. Sinking funds
    B. Junk bonds
    C. Serial bonds
    D. Unsecured bonds

17. Which of the following is considered equity?

    A. Lease
    B. Unsecured bond
    C. Secured bond
    D. Stock certificate

18. A _____ fund requires the issuer to retire some part of the bond issue prior to its maturity.

    A. sinking
    B. pension
    C. mutual
    D. federal

19. The monthly statistic which measures changes in the prices businesses pay for goods and services is the

    A. producer price index
    B. NASDAQ composite
    C. Dow Jones Industrial Average
    D. consumer price index

20. Which of the following is a form of inventory control?

    A. Capital budgeting
    B. Just–in–time
    C. Factoring
    D. Matching

21. A prediction of cash inflows and outflows in future periods is called a

    A. long–term forecast
    B. capital budget
    C. balance sheet
    D. cash flow forecast

22. A company which sells a piece of property in order to avoid the risks of ownership is an example of which risk control strategy?

    A. Loss reduction
    B. Risk–control transfer
    C. Loss prevention
    D. Risk avoidance

23. Paying off losses with monies that originate within the organization is an example of which risk–financing strategy?

    A. Risk retention
    B. Loss prevention
    C. Loss reduction
    D. Risk–financing transfer

24. The exchange of merchandise for merchandise is called

    A. exchange of goods
    B. commodity exchange
    C. barter
    D. dumping

25. The executive in charge of information and information systems in a corporation is the

    A. chief executive officer
    B. chief information officer
    C. chief financial officer
    D. president

KEY (CORRECT ANSWERS)

1. A
2. B
3. D
4. C
5. D

6. A
7. B
8. C
9. D
10. A

11. B
12. D
13. C
14. D
15. A

16. B
17. D
18. A
19. A
20. B

21. D
22. B
23. A
24. C
25. B

TEST 2

DIRECTIONS: Each question or incomplete statement is followed by several suggested answers or completions. Select the one that BEST answers the question or completes the statement. *PRINT THE LETTER OF THE CORRECT ANSWER IN THE SPACE AT THE RIGHT.*

1. Trying to buy insurance against the risk of an economic recession or depression is an example of a(n)

    A. loss reduction
    B. risk avoidance
    C. uninsurable risk
    D. insurable risk

    1.____

2. The demand for equal pay in jobs which require similar levels of education and training is called

    A. comparable worth
    B. affirmative action
    C. reverse discrimination
    D. corporate civil rights

    2.____

3. Which of the following is an example of a thrift institution?

    A. State bank
    B. Credit union
    C. Savings and loan
    D. All of the above

    3.____

4. Government, reseller, and industrial markets are all examples of

    A. consumer markets
    B. organizational markets
    C. target markets
    D. market segments

    4.____

5. When a business owner is responsible for all the debts of a business, so that even the owners' personal assets may be seized to satisfy claims against the business, then his/her liability is

    A. unlimited
    B. limited
    C. unsecured
    D. selective

    5.____

6. Under which of the following economic systems do citizens face the greatest degree of economic risk?

    A. Socialism
    B. Communism
    C. Capitalism
    D. Decentralized communism

    6.____

7. Insurance protecting against the failure of a second party to fulfill an obligation is a

    A. surety bond
    B. secured bond
    C. self–insurance policy
    D. secured loan

    7.____

8. Telecommuting is an example of _____ oriented motivational technique.

    A. employee
    B. job
    C. management
    D. organization

    8.____

9. That part of a firm's profits which goes to stockholders is called the

    A. bond
    B. stock
    C. stock split
    D. dividend

    9.____

10. A statement that describes the type of person best suited for a job is a

    A. job analysis
    B. resume
    C. job specification
    D. job description

    10.____

21

11. Dividing the market into specific user categories is called 11._____
    A. subfranchising   B. test marketing
    C. market segmentation   D. volume segmentation

12. The Organization of Petroleum–Exporting Countries (OPEC) is an example of a(n) 12._____
    A. producer cartel   B. multinational corporation
    C. management cartel   D. international union

13. Analyzing the market, setting objectives, assessing resources, and developing a strategy are all stages of 13._____
    A. target marketing   B. market segmentation
    C. the marketing mix   D. the market–planning process

14. Funds raised from borrowing money through the sale of bonds or from banks is called 14._____
    A. equity capital   B. debt capital
    C. revenue   D. secured bonds

15. The lowest rate of interest which banks charge to their customers is called the _____ rate. 15._____
    A. market   B. discount
    C. prime interest   D. Federal funds

16. Limits on the amount of money that banks and stockbrokers can lend customers for buying stocks are called 16._____
    A. margin requirements   B. reserve requirements
    C. open–market operations   D. selective credit controls

17. Economists who advocate lowering taxes to increase investment in production, in order to increase production activity and decrease unemployment are practicing 17._____
    A. macroeconomics   B. supply–side economics
    C. open–market regulation   D. microeconomics

18. Attempting to create the impression in the minds of consumers that one product is superior to others is an example of 18._____
    A. target marketing   B. market segmentation
    C. product modification   D. product differentiation

19. Nonprofit insurance companies owned by policyholders are called 19._____
    A. environmental insurers   B. private insurance companies
    C. mutual companies   D. stock companies

20. A name, symbol or design which identifies and distinguishes the goods of one seller from another is called a 20._____
    A. brand   B. brand name
    C. product   D. franchise

21. Which of the following is considered a transfer payment?   21.____

    A. State police force   B. Food stamps
    C. Stock dividend   D. Capital gains tax

22. An agreement which grants a person living in a foreign market the right to oversee franchise operations in that market is called a   22.____

    A. partnership agreement   B. market order
    C. franchising agreement   D. subfranchising agreement

23. Working to figure out what product consumers want, what types of packaging consumers prefer, and what types of selling practices are most likely to appeal to them are goals of   23.____

    A. the market planning process
    B. the marketing mix
    C. market research
    D. market segmentation

24. A wholesaler who solicits orders from retailers and other wholesalers and then has merchandise shipped directly from producers to buyers is a   24.____

    A. drop shipper   B. broker
    C. corporate entrepreneur   D. truck jobber

25. Which of the following is a disadvantage of franchising?   25.____

    A. High risk   B. Monthly royalty
    C. Low name recognition   D. Lack of advertising

KEY (CORRECT ANSWERS)

1.	C	11.	D
2.	A	12.	A
3.	D	13.	D
4.	B	14.	B
5.	A	15.	C
6.	C	16.	A
7.	A	17.	B
8.	B	18.	D
9.	D	19.	C
10.	C	20.	A

21. B
22. D
23. C
24. A
25. B

EXAMINATION SECTION
TEST 1

DIRECTIONS: Each question or incomplete statement is followed by several suggested answers or completions. Select the one that BEST answers the question or completes the statement. *PRINT THE LETTER OF THE CORRECT ANSWER IN THE SPACE AT THE RIGHT.*

1. A brand which has received legal protection for its name and design is called a   1.____

    A. trademark
    B. patent
    C. franchise
    D. product

2. Management information systems generally serve   2.____

    A. operating personnel
    B. office staff
    C. executives
    D. middle managers

3. The process of creating the instructions which direct computers use to perform certain jobs is called   3.____

    A. microprocessing
    B. programming
    C. integrated circuitry
    D. software engineering

4. Adding product lines to a store when those product lines are not usually carried there is called   4.____

    A. exclusive distribution
    B. the push strategy
    C. scrambled merchandising
    D. intensive distribution

5. The organization which serves as a deposit for the excess of Federal Reserve District banks is called the Federal   5.____

    A. Deposit Insurance Corporation
    B. Trade Commission
    C. Savings and Loan Insurance Corporation
    D. Reserve System

6. What is the primary difference between transactional leadership and transformational leadership?   6.____

    A. Transactional inspires employees to perform as expected and transformational inspires employees to go beyond the expected levels of performance.
    B. Transformational relies on a strict adherence to stated policies.
    C. Transactional relies on de-centralized authority.
    D. Transformational inspires employees to perform as expected and transactional inspires employees to go beyond the expected levels of performance.

7. An agreement to bring in an impartial third party to render a binding decision in a labor dispute is called   7.____

    A. an agency shop agreement
    B. collective bargaining
    C. arbitration
    D. an injunction

25

8. Which of the following is an advantage partnerships have over sole proprietorships?

   A. Partnerships have limited liability
   B. Generally higher credit ratings
   C. Independent decision-making, no need to consult with co-owners
   D. Less red tape in getting started

9. This term refers to the purchase and sale of goods for immediate delivery.

   A. Spot markets   B. Push strategy
   C. Scrambled merchandising D. Selective distribution

10. The idea of selling more goods to other nations than a country buys is called

    A. hedging   B. mercantilism
    C. trade protectionism D. supply-side economics

11. Which of the following is NOT a protectionist measure?

    A. Tariffs
    B. Quotas
    C. Boycott of goods due to political protest
    D. Embargo

12. A distribution system in which all the organizations in the channel are owned by one firm is a(n) _____ distribution system.

    A. contracted B. exclusive
    C. intensive   D. corporate

13. In their professional relationships with others, what roles are managers expected to fulfill?

    I. Leadership
    II. Liaison
    III. Informational
    IV. Decision-making

    The CORRECT answer is:

    A. I, II, III   B. II, III, IV
    C. I, II, IV   D. I, II, III, IV

14. A provision in a negotiated labor-management contract that stipulates that employees who benefit from a union must either join or pay dues to the union is called a(n)

    A. yellow-dog contract   B. union security clause
    C. agency shop agreement D. union shop agreement

15. Dividing the market into submarkets with similar characteristics is called _____ segmentation.

    A. volume B. demographic
    C. market D. geographic

16. The amount of effort put forth by a worker depends on the expected outcome. This statement expresses which of the following theories?

    A. Motivational hygiene B. Classical
    C. Piecework   D. Expectancy

17. The organization in a channel that gets the other members to cooperate is called a   17.____

    A. channel captain   B. channel of distribution
    C. containerization   D. volume segmentation

18. A manager who delegates authority and involves employees in decision-making is using   18.____
    which style of management?

    A. Transformational   B. Laissez-faire
    C. Autocratic   D. Democratic

19. Preferred stock that accumulates unpaid dividends is called _____ stock.   19.____

    A. preferred   B. common
    C. cumulative preferred   D. blue-chip

20. Some cosmetic companies use the home-party approach to distribute their products   20.____
    directly to the consumer. This kind of distribution is part of which aspect of the marketing
    mix?

    A. Product   B. Price
    C. Promotion   D. Place

21. Marketing middlemen who assist buyers and sellers in negotiating an exchange are   21.____
    called

    A. brokers   B. arbitrators
    C. drop shippers   D. wholesalers

22. The use of information which a person has gained through his/her position which allows   22.____
    him/her to benefit from fluctuations in the stock market is called

    A. inventory financing   B. insider trading
    C. incubating   D. venture capitalizing

23. Unlimited liability means   23.____

    A. the business is liable to stockholders for all debts and damages
    B. the owners are not personally liable for business debts
    C. the owners are liable for any business debt that does not exceed the owner's origi-
       nal investment
    D. any debts attributable to the business can also be attached to the owner

24. A professional who coordinates all the marketing efforts for a particular product or brand 24.____
    is termed a _____ manager.

    A. supervisory   B. top
    C. product   D. participative

25. Which of the following is a characteristic of a quasi-public corporation?   25.____

    A. Trades stock on the open market
    B. Government-granted monopoly
    C. Owned by private individuals
    D. Formed by the government for a specific purpose

KEY (CORRECT ANSWERS)

1.	A		11.	C
2.	D		12.	D
3.	B		13.	D
4.	C		14.	B
5.	D		15.	C
6.	A		16.	D
7.	C		17.	A
8.	B		18.	D
9.	A		19.	C
10.	B		20.	D

21. A
22. B
23. D
24. C
25. B

TEST 2

DIRECTIONS: Each question or incomplete statement is followed by several suggested answers or completions. Select the one that BEST answers the question or completes the statement. *PRINT THE LETTER OF THE CORRECT ANSWER IN THE SPACE AT THE RIGHT.*

1. The Dow Jones Industrial Average reports

   A. the average cost of 30 industrial stocks
   B. over the counter trades
   C. changes in the prices of 400 goods and services
   D. annual union dues

2. Which of the following is the responsibility of middle managers?

   A. Directly oversee the work of operating employees
   B. Develop plans to implement the goals of top managers
   C. Take overall responsibility for the organization
   D. Coordinate the work of the top managers

3. An organization that seeks profits by providing needed goods and services is called a

   A. corporation   B. partnership
   C. business   D. firm

4. Import taxes intended to raise the price of imports so that domestic products will have an advantage are called

   A. protective tariffs   B. primary boycotts
   C. embargo   D. closed-shop agreements

5. A checking account is a

   A. mutual fund   B. negotiable instrument
   C. demand deposit   D. time deposit

6. A person who works in a corporation and takes responsibility for creating innovation and launching new products is a(n)

   A. internal marketer   B. marketing manager
   C. entrepreneur   D. intrapreneur

7. The formation of monopolies is discouraged by

   A. recession   B. government intervention
   C. low inflation   D. low unemployment

8. The joining of unrelated firms is called a

   A. vertical merger   B. horizontal merger
   C. conglomerate merger   D. leveraged buyout

9. Which of the following is an example of a not-for-profit corporation?

   A. Princeton University   B. Pacific Gas and Electric
   C. Microsoft   D. AT&T

10. Selling products for less money in a foreign country than it costs to produce them in the producing country is known as

    A. piggybacking
    B. dumping
    C. drop shipping
    D. skunkworking

11. Utilitarianism states that the right decision is the one that

    A. produces the least degree of harm
    B. produces an equal distribution of burdens and benefits
    C. does not violate the rights of any individual
    D. achieves the greatest good for the greatest number of people

12. A financial plan which allocates resources based on projected revenues is called a

    A. balance sheet
    B. budget
    C. business plan
    D. break-even analysis

13. Responsibilities for a business's losses only up to the amount of the original investment is called

    A. strict liability
    B. rule of indemnity
    C. limited liability
    D. unlimited liability

14. When two firms form one company, it is called a

    A. merger
    B. vertical merger
    C. horizontal merger
    D. hostile takeover

15. The number of products consumers are willing to buy at a specific price and time is called

    A. the equilibrium point
    B. the market price
    C. supply
    D. demand

16. When consumers have several similar products to choose from, then competition between these products will be based on
    I. quality
    II. quantity
    III. customer satisfaction

    The CORRECT answer is:

    A. II, III
    B. I, III
    C. I, II
    D. I, II, III

17. Efficiency which results from employee specialization is called

    A. containerization
    B. human resource management
    C. economy of scale
    D. factoring

18. The technology industry in Country A accuses the technology industry in Country B of selling computer chips at a price below their cost in order to break into Country A's market. This practice is an example of

    A. countertrading
    B. dumping
    C. exporting
    D. trade protectionism

19. What are the 4 P's of marketing?

    A. Product, placement, process, promotion
    B. Price, placement, promotion, profit
    C. Product, price, promotion, profit
    D. Product, price, placement, promotion

20. A pre-employment psychological test is used to identify

    A. interests
    B. eye-hand coordination
    C. presence of illegal substances in the blood
    D. specific job skills

21. A ban on the import or export of certain products is called a(n)

    A. boycott
    C. embargo
    B. closed-shop agreement
    D. monopoly

22. Inflation caused by too much demand for goods and services is

    A. demand-pull inflation
    C. stagflation
    B. cost-push inflation
    D. recession

23. Which of the following is considered an incentive-based compensation program?
    I. Bonus
    II. Commission
    III. Salary
    IV. Goal sharing

    The CORRECT answer is:

    A. I, II, III
    C. II, IV
    B. II, III, IV
    D. I, II, IV

24. Within the _____ economic system, resources are allocated partially by the market and partially by the government.

    A. capitalist
    C. communist
    B. socialist
    D. oligopolist

25. A group of people who meet to discuss their reactions to an organization and/or its products is called

    A. a focus group
    C. franchise wholesalers
    B. marketing middlemen
    D. an entrepreneurial team

KEY (CORRECT ANSWERS)

1. A
2. B
3. C
4. A
5. C

6. D
7. B
8. C
9. A
10. B

11. D
12. B
13. C
14. A
15. D

16. B
17. C
18. B
19. D
20. A

21. C
22. A
23. D
24. B
25. A

EXAMINATION SECTION
TEST 1

DIRECTIONS: Each question or incomplete statement is followed by several suggested answers or completions. Select the one that BEST answers the question or completes the statement. *PRINT THE LETTER OF THE CORRECT ANSWER IN THE SPACE AT THE RIGHT.*

1. An advantage of forming a business plan is that it

    A. is a necessary part of *going public*
    B. ensures that no one steals your business idea
    C. is helpful in order to obtain outside financing
    D. protects against unlimited liability

    1.____

2. A distribution system in which all retail-level marketing functions are managed by producers is called a(n) _____ distribution system.

    A. corporate
    B. channel of
    C. contractual
    D. administered

    2.____

3. The study of the behavior of people in specific markets is called

    A. macroeconomics
    B. microeconomics
    C. market segmentation
    D. market targeting

    3.____

4. Compensation based on an employee's acquisition of new skills is termed

    A. profit-sharing
    B. goal-sharing
    C. knowledge-based pay
    D. pay for performance

    4.____

5. An organization owned by members who pay an annual membership fee and share in any profits is a(n)

    A. partnership
    B. cooperative
    C. S corporation
    D. limited partnership

    5.____

6. The total output of goods and services divided by work hours equals

    A. profit
    B. trial balance
    C. assets
    D. productivity

    6.____

7. If a company needs to adjust to a shrinking business, but wants to avoid massive layoffs, it should

    A. restructure
    B. terminate
    C. outplace
    D. downsize

    7.____

8. Which term refers to innovative, entrepreneurial units operating on the margins of a corporation?

    A. Truck jobber
    B. Rack jobber
    C. Skunkworks
    D. Piggyback

    8.____

9. One of the basic assumptions of Management Theory Y is that the average person

    A. wants security above all else
    B. feels that work is as natural as rest or play

    9.____

C. wishes to be directed
D. dislikes work

10. The right to use a business's name and sell its products in a given area is called a

    A. franchise
    B. franchise agreement
    C. target market
    D. marketing mix

11. Which of the following techniques is used to control inventory?

    A. Hard manufacturing
    B. Repetitive manufacturing
    C. Material requirements planning
    D. Flexible manufacturing

12. An entity which resembles a corporation, but which is taxed like a partnership, is called a(n)

    A. limited partnership
    B. small business
    C. savings and loan
    D. S corporation

13. The study and use of ergonomics is an example of

    A. methods improvement
    B. the just-in-time system
    C. material requirements planning
    D. quality assurance

14. An agreement which allows employers to hire anyone, but which employees must pay union fees even though they do not have the right to join unions, is called a(n) _____ agreement.

    A. closed-shop
    B. agency shop
    C. collective bargaining
    D. franchise

15. An example of a consumer market is a

    A. copy machine company who sells machines to corporations
    B. clothing company who sells to department stores
    C. furniture company which specializes in office furniture for businesses
    D. furniture store which specializes in home office and conventional furniture

16. The idea that a country should produce and sell to other countries those products that it produces most efficiently is called

    A. comparative advantage
    B. absolute advantage
    C. extrinsic reward
    D. competition-oriented pricing

17. The rise of fast-food restaurants devoted to healthier eating is an example of a company responding to which aspect of the external environment?

    A. Competition
    B. Economic forces
    C. Technology
    D. Social trends

18. Wrongful conduct which results in injury to another person's body, property or reputation is called

    A. tort
    B. strict liability
    C. rule of indemnity
    D. statutory grievance

19. The influence of family members, friends, and colleagues are examples of which aspect of buyer behavior?

    A. Situational factors
    B. Reference groups
    C. Culture
    D. Social class

20. Utilizing a high-quality image in order to convey status, increase desirability, and charge more for a product is part of which aspect of the marketing mix?

    A. Product
    B. Place
    C. Price
    D. Promotion

21. A person with entrepreneurial skills who works in a corporation to launch new products is called a(n)

    A. corporate entrepreneur
    B. start-up
    C. entrepreneurial manager
    D. intrapreneur

22. Targeting consumers in Hawaii and Florida as potential purchasers of a new suntan lotion is an example of which type of market segmentation?

    A. Psychographic
    B. Behavioral
    C. Geographic
    D. Demographic

23. A _____ provides the issuer of a bond the right to retire the bond before it matures.

    A. call provision
    B. closed-shop agreement
    C. convertible bond
    D. debenture bond

24. A demand deposit is an example of

    A. plastic money
    B. a time deposit
    C. M1
    D. M2

25. Using accounts receivable as security is called

    A. hedging
    B. pledging
    C. inventory financing
    D. factoring

KEY (CORRECT ANSWERS)

1.	C		11.	C
2.	D		12.	D
3.	B		13.	A
4.	C		14.	B
5.	B		15.	D
6.	D		16.	A
7.	A		17.	D
8.	C		18.	A
9.	B		19.	B
10.	A		20.	C

21. D
22. C
23. A
24. C
25. B

TEST 2

DIRECTIONS: Each question or incomplete statement is followed by several suggested answers or completions. Select the one that BEST answers the question or completes the statement. *PRINT THE LETTER OF THE CORRECT ANSWER IN THE SPACE AT THE RIGHT.*

1. The business to whom a check is written is the 1.____
   - A. time depositor
   - B. demand depositor
   - C. payor
   - D. payee

2. Net sales minus the cost of goods sold equals the 2.____
   - A. income statement
   - B. gross margin
   - C. balance of payments
   - D. gross national product

3. A nonprofit member-owned cooperative offering checking and savings accounts and consumer loans is called a 3.____
   - A. credit union
   - B. savings and loan
   - C. savings bank
   - D. state bank

4. When a person buys stocks by borrowing some of the purchase cost from the broker, they are 4.____
   - A. diversifying
   - B. dumping
   - C. buying on margin
   - D. countertrading

5. A series of points on a graph which shows the relationship between price and quantity supplied is the 5.____
   - A. demand
   - B. equilibrium price
   - C. demand curve
   - D. supply curve

6. Buying and selling in the futures market equal and opposite to what the buyer currently has is called 6.____
   - A. factoring
   - B. pledging
   - C. hedging
   - D. speculating

7. Which of the following measures can a country take to protect its industries from importers? 7.____
   - A. Tariffs
   - B. Boycotts
   - C. Absolute advantage measures
   - D. Comparative advantage measures

8. Which of the following is likely to produce pressures causing management practices to become more innovative? 8.____
   - A. Elimination of trading blocs
   - B. Demographic shifts
   - C. Increases in the GNP
   - D. Depression or recession

9. Which pricing method assigns high prices to products in order to make optimum profit while there is little or no competition?

   A. Competition-oriented pricing
   B. Demand-oriented pricing
   C. Exclusive distribution
   D. Skimming price strategy

10. The Gross Domestic Product includes the _____ goods and services produced by the economy.

   A. dollar value of all
   B. total value of all reported and unreported
   C. dollar value of all reported and unreported
   D. total value of all

11. Which form of business ownership is the easiest and least expensive to start?

   A. Franchise
   B. Partnership
   C. Sole proprietorship
   D. Corporation

12. The pricing strategy based on consumer demand is called

   A. competition-oriented pricing
   B. demand-oriented pricing
   C. demand-pull inflation
   D. cost-push inflation

13. Which of the following are forms of partnership?
   I. General
   II. Limited
   III. Corporate
   IV. Master limited

   The CORRECT answer is:
   A. I, II, IV
   B. I, II, III
   C. II, III, IV
   D. I, II, III, IV

14. Which of the following are common categories for financing a small business?
   I. Venture capitalists
   II. Debt financing
   III. Public stock offerings
   IV. Equity financing

   The CORRECT answer is:
   A. I, II
   B. II, IV
   C. I, II, III
   D. I, II, III, IV

15. When manufacturers advertise to wholesalers and retailers, it is called

   A. internal marketing
   B. test marketing
   C. trade advertising
   D. subfranchise marketing

16. Deciding to buy a book because of its placement in a prominent place in the bookstore is an example of which aspect of buyer behavior?

    A. Culture
    B. Situational factor
    C. Social class
    D. Self-image

17. When two firms join in the same industry, it is called a

    A. merger
    B. hostile takeover
    C. vertical merger
    D. horizontal merger

18. Personal computers are examples of

    A. workstations
    B. mainframe computers
    C. microcomputers
    D. minicomputers

19. The most basic form of ownership of firms is called _____ stock.

    A. common   B. blue-chip   C. income   D. preferred

20. Computer systems which are required to process new information instantly use _____ processing.

    A. micro   B. real-time   C. batch   D. parallel

21. A computer system which imitates the thought processes of a human expert in a particular field is using

    A. a microprocessor
    B. a language processor
    C. artificial intelligence
    D. an expert system

22. Employment activities which give preference to females and minorities in an attempt to *right past wrongs* is called

    A. affirmative action
    B. fringe benefits
    C. right-to-work laws
    D. public relations

23. Which of the following are among the index of leading economic indicators?
    I. Stock market
    II. Housing starts
    III. Length of workweek
    IV. Consumer confidence

The CORRECT answer is:
    A. I, II
    B. I, II, IV
    C. II, III, IV
    D. I, II, III, IV

24. The records system which allows information from accounting journals to be categorized so that managers can find all the information about a single account in one place is a

    A. balance sheet
    B. ledger
    C. business plan
    D. budget sheet

25. Country A exported $2 million of goods in 1998, and imported $1 million. The $1 million difference is known as the

   A. balance of payments
   B. trade deficit
   C. balance of trade
   D. trade surplus

25.____

KEY (CORRECT ANSWERS)

1. D
2. B
3. A
4. C
5. D

6. C
7. A
8. B
9. D
10. A

11. C
12. B
13. A
14. B
15. C

16. B
17. D
18. C
19. A
20. B

21. D
22. A
23. B
24. B
25. D

EXAMINATION SECTION
TEST 1

DIRECTIONS: Each question or incomplete statement is followed by several suggested answers or completions. Select the one that BEST answers the question or completes the statement. *PRINT THE LETTER OF THE CORRECT ANSWER IN THE SPACE AT THE RIGHT.*

1. The legislation that eliminated several forms of price discrimination that had given large businesses a competitive advantage over smaller businesses was the _____ Act. 1._____

    A. Sherman Antitrust
    B. Federal Trade Commission
    C. Clayton
    D. Interstate Commerce

2. Which of the following investments has the highest potential for income? 2._____

    A. Common stock
    B. Money market account
    C. Savings account
    D. Preferred stock

3. The manufacturing of steel is an example of 3._____

    A. analytic system
    B. synthetic system
    C. distillation process
    D. flexible manufacturing

4. For each pay period, payroll records do NOT typically record 4._____

    A. deductions
    B. gross earnings
    C. net earnings
    D. total hours worked

5. _____ is the use of borrowed money to make more money. 5._____

    A. Leverage
    B. The matching principle
    C. Capital budgeting
    D. Cash flow

6. In order to identify students who may need extra assistance or who have been misplaced, it is most helpful, in the first days of the class, for a business teacher to distribute 6._____

    A. the text and have students fill out a questionnaire about their level of comfort with the text
    B. a questionnaire about what prior knowledge students might have about the business curriculum
    C. the text and have students answer open-ended questions about the text in writing
    D. a multiple-choice *pretest* designed to assess a student's prior knowledge and skill level within the business curriculum

7. Each of the following is a function of management EXCEPT 7._____

    A. controlling
    B. financing
    C. directing
    D. planning

8. After the delivery of a curriculum about business, it is important for all students to be able to do each of the following EXCEPT 8._____

    A. develop personal skills related to business occupations
    B. improve the understanding of business and its relation to the total economy

C. develop occupational skills to market, merchandise, and manage the flow of goods and services
D. develop personal consumer competence and to relate the role of the consumer to the total economy

9. Corporations

   A. exist only in contemplation of the law
   B. are tangible in the eyes of the law
   C. are the business owners
   D. are visible according to the law

10. In business accounting, a journal

    A. includes only credit entries
    B. is where miscellaneous accounts are kept
    C. usually includes a balance column
    D. is a book of original entry

11. In business, a *narrow* span of control works best when

    A. the manager has few responsibilities outside of supervision
    B. subordinates are located near each other
    C. new and different problems often arise
    D. there is little interaction required between management and workers

12. On what document can the record of a firm's liabilities, assets, and owner's equity be found?

    A. Income statement   B. Journal
    C. Trial balance   D. Balance sheet

13. The index of leading economic indicators is a

    A. set of variables used by a company to measure its financial wealth
    B. composite of broad measures of economic activity used to predict changes in the business cycle
    C. single variable used to predict future governmental activity
    D. scale used to determine the current level of economic activity

14. In a typical business curriculum, which of the following units would be taught FIRST?

    A. Credit   B. Spending
    C. Investment   D. Income

15. The PRIMARY difference between an executive information system (EIS) and a decision support system (DDS) is that the EIS

    A. makes upper-level decisions
    B. organizes the necessary information to assist decision-making
    C. is used for complex, one-of-a-kind decisions
    D. has a more strategic focus

16. The socioeconomic model includes each of the following ideas EXCEPT that   16.____

    A. voluntary involvement can prevent government involvement
    B. resources are available to tackle complex social problems
    C. corporate money, time, and talent should be used to maximize profits
    D. solving social problems can lead to long-term profitability

17. Warranties, trade names, and packaging are concerns of _____ ingredients.   17.____

    A. distribution   B. product
    C. promotion   D. pricing

18. Each of the following is an advantage associated with division departmentalization   18.____
    EXCEPT

    A. offering a higher degree of flexibility
    B. allowing better coordination across different divisions
    C. allowing a higher degree of focus on problem areas
    D. providing a higher level of customer service

19. Each of the following is an advantage associated with promoting human resources from   19.____
    within EXCEPT

    A. greater success in finding the best employee
    B. greater morale
    C. reduced orientation requirements
    D. lower recruiting costs

20. The basis of _____ theory is the development of an outcome-to-income ratio.   20.____

    A. reinforcement   B. equity
    C. quality circles   D. expectancy

21. Which of the following is a characteristic of the full-block letter style?   21.____

    A. Inside address written below the final line of the signature
    B. No indentations
    C. Date line flush with the right margin
    D. Omits salutation and complimentary close

22. _____ is a type of liability insurance that covers losses occurring during the policy   22.____
    period, regardless of when the claim is made.

    A. Contingent business   B. No-fault
    C. Claims-made   D. Occurrence

23. Which of the following statements is true of visual learners?   23.____

    A. They benefit most from the application of rich and varied colors in visual aids.
    B. Although they tend to learn quickly, they also tend to forget quickly.
    C. They are poorer readers than other students on the average.
    D. If they hear something, they are not likely to remember it.

24. Machines, tools, and buildings used to produce goods and services, as well as the money that buys other resources, are known as

    A. assets
    B. raw materials
    C. natural resources
    D. capital

25. To be insurable, a risk's potential losses must be

    A. predictable
    B. immeasurable
    C. centrally located
    D. under the insured's control

KEY (CORRECT ANSWERS)

1. C	11. C
2. D	12. D
3. B	13. B
4. C	14. D
5. A	15. D
6. C	16. C
7. B	17. B
8. C	18. B
9. A	19. A
10. D	20. B

21. B
22. C
23. B
24. D
25. A

TEST 2

DIRECTIONS: Each question or incomplete statement is followed by several suggested answers or completions. Select the one that BEST answers the question or completes the statement. *PRINT THE LETTER OF THE CORRECT ANSWER IN THE SPACE AT THE RIGHT.*

1. At most companies, the public-relations director and the personnel manager are   1.____

    A. top managers
    B. staff personnel
    C. middle managers
    D. line personnel

2. When addressing a business envelope, any account numbers should be written on the _____ line of the address block.   2.____

    A. first
    B. second
    C. next to last
    D. last

3. Currently, union members are seeking the nontraditional goal of   3.____

    A. more involvement in decision-making
    B. greater job security
    C. higher wages
    D. greater job safety

4. When arranging a business trip, which of the following should generally be performed FIRST?   4.____

    A. Submit a time-and-route schedule
    B. Assembling data and supplies to be taken on trip
    C. Making financial arrangements for the trip
    D. Preparing travel itinerary and appointment schedule

5. Nationwide, the ratio of state banks to national banks is approximately   5.____

    A. 1:2
    B. 1:1
    C. 2:1
    D. 4:1

6. When a company exercises the right to pay off a bond before it matures, it is dealing with _____ bonds.   6.____

    A. junk
    B. term
    C. callable
    D. convertible

7. Economic education is related to the goal of distributive education in several ways. Which of the following is NOT a statement of an important relationship between the two?   7.____

    A. Economic analysis is a necessary ingredient of distributive education if educators are to meet their social and economic responsibilities.
    B. Understanding the role of marketing is essential to the knowledge of economics.
    C. Economic understanding is essential for an appreciation of the importance of personal use skills in business.
    D. Economic understanding is a necessary fortification for determining effective marketing practices.

45

8. The two MAJOR ways to finance small businesses in the United States are

   A. personal savings and loans from friends
   B. debt financing and equity financing
   C. issuing stock and bank loans
   D. small business loans and family loans

9. Which of the following statements about profit is TRUE?

   A. Business profit becomes the property of the owner.
   B. It generally involves low risk.
   C. A business must make a profit every year to continue operating.
   D. Large companies usually make the largest profits.

10. What type of mutual fund apportions investments among common stocks, bonds, and preferred stocks?

    A. Growth income
    B. Income
    C. Balanced
    D. Growth

11. The term for a contract endorsement that consists *only* of the payee's signature is _____ endorsement.

    A. qualified
    B. restrictive
    C. blank
    D. special

12. In a management-by-objectives (MBO) program, the _____ would occur first.

    A. endorsement of the program by top management
    B. review of progress by manager and subordinates
    C. establishment of preliminary goals
    D. assignment of certain goals to subordinates by the manager

13. Long-term financing should be used by a business for

    A. purchasing inventory for resale
    B. paying utilities
    C. developing and marketing new products
    D. paying salaries

14. Which of the following statements about the organizational buying process is FALSE?

    A. It involves larger quantities.
    B. It takes less time to plan the purchase.
    C. On average, it involves higher dollar amounts.
    D. It is more likely to involve customized product design.

15. Under the terms of a _____ insurance policy, the insurance company agrees to pay the amount due on a loan if the insured dies.

    A. credit life
    B. pension plan
    C. loss of earning power
    D. surety bond

16. The improvement of quality control in order to lower the probability of a lawsuit based on an unsafe product is
an example of the risk _____ approach to risk management.

    A. assumption
    B. transfer
    C. avoidance
    D. reduction

17. Under the terms of current patent law, patents are granted for a term of

    A. 10 years
    B. 17 years
    C. 30 years
    D. a lifetime

18. Convenience products

    A. are purchased infrequently
    B. have an easily recognizable image developed by advertising
    C. are purchased after considerable thought
    D. have no acceptable substitute to the consumer

19. Operations managers would be most concerned with

    A. union activities
    B. target markets
    C. coordination of information
    D. new technology

20. The _____ model of social responsibility includes the traditional concept that businesses are responsible to their investors, and that social responsibility is someone else's role.

    A. socioeconomic
    B. collectivist
    C. corporate
    D. economic

21. A business course includes a series of lessons designed to teach that individuals and families receive income from three basic sources. Each of the following student activities will probably be helpful in teaching this principle EXCEPT

    A. telling where their families get the money they receive
    B. tracing each of their own sources of income through a flow chart
    C. listing job satisfactions other than financial reward gained from working
    D. proposing as many ways as possible in which a person might increase her income from each of the major sources

22. Each of the following is an advantage of the line organization EXCEPT the

    A. quickness with which decisions can be made
    B. simplicity of the organization
    C. distribution of decision-making authority
    D. tendency to lower expenses

23. What is the legal term for a close, mutual, or successive relationship to the same right of property or the power to enforce a promise or warranty?

    A. Binder
    B. Privity
    C. Writ
    D. Trust

24. Which of the following is an action the Federal Reserve would undertake in order to reduce the nation's money supply?

    A. Sell government bonds
    B. Borrow from foreign governments
    C. Lower the discount rate
    D. Reduce reserve requirements

25. Current assets - current liabilities =

    A. quick ratio
    B. working capital
    C. return on equity
    D. net profit margin

KEY (CORRECT ANSWERS)

1.	B	11.	C
2.	A	12.	A
3.	A	13.	C
4.	A	14.	B
5.	C	15.	A
6.	C	16.	D
7.	C	17.	B
8.	B	18.	B
9.	A	19.	D
10.	C	20.	D

21.	C
22.	C
23.	B
24.	A
25.	B

TEST 3

DIRECTIONS: Each question or incomplete statement is followed by several suggested answers or completions. Select the one that BEST answers the question or completes the statement. *PRINT THE LETTER OF THE CORRECT ANSWER IN THE SPACE AT THE RIGHT.*

1. Approximately _____ of the United States' Gross National Product is made up of consumer goods.　　1.____

   A. 1/4　　B. 1/2　　C. 2/3　　D. 3/4

2. _____ bankruptcy is the term for the action when a bank loaning funds to a company initiates bankruptcy proceedings.　　2.____

   A. Involuntary　　　　　　　B. Reorganization
   C. Cost minimization　　　　D. Voluntary

3. To make up for an underpayment, a company's purchasing agent must submit a check for 70 cents to a supplier. Which of the following best shows how the check should be filled out?　　3.____

   A. Ø and 75/100 .... Dollars
   B. 75/100 .... Dollars
   C. Only Seventy-five Cents
   D. 75¢ .... Dollars

4. What is the major goal of a planned economy?　　4.____

   A. Social quality
   B. Minimized suffering
   C. Redistribution of money from wealthy to poor
   D. Maximized production capacity

5. An employee's _____ rights are insured by having a grievance procedure so the employee can have an opportunity to present his or her side of a situation.　　5.____

   A. injunction　　　B. due process
   C. mediation　　　D. arbitration

6. _____ skills reflect the knowledge required in a particular job.　　6.____

   A. Analytical　　　B. Diagnostic
   C. Conceptual　　D. Technical

7. A piece of paper attached to a negotiable instrument that provides space to write endorsements when there is no room on the instrument itself is known as a(n)　　7.____

   A. buffer　　　　B. writ of attachment
   C. allonge　　　D. hedge

8. What is the term for creating the desired place for a product in the mind of the market?　　8.____

   A. Positioning　　B. Advertising
   C. Segmenting　　D. Public relations

49

9. In a unit on credit, the following principle is introduced: An individual or family may borrow money or obtain goods and services on credit from many sources. Which of the following student activities would be LEAST useful for exploring this principle?

   A. Discussing how institutional costs such as paperwork and overhead might affect the annual rate of interest for very small loans
   B. Discussing the details and impact of truth-in-lending laws on creditors and consumers
   C. Collecting information about several institutions in the community that extend credit
   D. Giving examples of the opportunity costs involved in the use of credit

10. A(n) _____ occurs when an administrative agency allows a company to stop doing something without admitting any illegal behavior.

    A. cessation order
    B. administrative opinion
    C. neutrality decree
    D. consent order

11. Which of the following behaviors is MOST likely to lead to the establishment of good credit?

    A. Avoiding all credit cards
    B. Taking out a small installment loan at a bank
    C. Disregarding small balances on department store accounts, and concentrating on large debt amounts first
    D. Borrowing from a small-loan company

12. Which of the following basic understandings should a student acquire LAST in a unit on spending?

    A. Some consumer spending is for fixed expenditures, while other spending is discretionary.
    B. Through its effect on production and employment, consumer spending helps to determine the total income of the economy.
    C. In planning her spending, it may be helpful for an individual to know how all consumers together spend their income.
    D. In addition to spending for goods and services that directly satisfy wants, a consumer may buy insurance to protect himself and his family from future economic loss.

13. A signed statement by the person who executes a legal instrument that the instrument is genuine is known as a(n)

    A. attestation
    B. deposition
    C. acknowledgement
    D. notarization

14. The type of products that typically involve the highest level of brand loyalty are _____ goods.

    A. unsought
    B. shopping
    C. convenience
    D. specialty

15. A building is considered to be a(n) _____ asset.

    A. intangible
    B. current
    C. variable
    D. fixed

16. Which of the following is NOT a type of layout used for production routing?

    A. Assembly-line
    B. Fixed-position
    C. Process
    D. Service-line

17. Under pure competition, there is a price at which the quantity of a good or service demanded is exactly equal to the quantity supplied. This price is known as the _____ price.

    A. retail   B. market   C. purchase   D. fixed

18. Currency and demand deposits compose the _____ measure of money.

    A. M_1 B. M_2 C. M_3 D. L

19. In a formal report, which of the following elements would appear FIRST?

    A. Notes
    B. Abstract
    C. Letter of transmittal
    D. Introduction

20. An *organic* business structure

    A. uses a narrow span of management
    B. involves a high level of job specialization
    C. tends to have generalized and informal delegation patterns
    D. has clearly outlined line and staff positions

21. The production of more chemical and radioactive waste by modern technology makes _____ pollution a serious problem.

    A. environmental
    B. land
    C. water
    D. air

22. A _____ merger is one in which a company involved in one phase of a business absorbs or joins a company involved in another phase of that business.

    A. corporate
    B. horizontal
    C. vertical
    D. conglomerate

23. Purchasers of GNP can be grouped into each of the following categories EXCEPT

    A. foreign expenditures
    B. business expenditure for investment
    C. individual consumer expenditures
    D. government subsidies

24. Fourth-generation computer languages

    A. communicate with words similar to the functions to be performed
    B. communicate in terms of what the computer is to do, rather than what the user wants done
    C. use 1's and 0's to communicate
    D. use mnemonic codes to communicate

25. _____ managers are supervisory managers.

   A. Upper-level
   B. Line
   C. Operating
   D. Middle

KEY (CORRECT ANSWERS)

1.	C	11.	B
2.	A	12.	C
3.	C	13.	C
4.	A	14.	D
5.	B	15.	D
6.	D	16.	D
7.	C	17.	B
8.	A	18.	A
9.	D	19.	C
10.	D	20.	C

21. B
22. C
23. D
24. A
25. C

EXAMINATION SECTION
TEST 1

DIRECTIONS: Each question or incomplete statement is followed by several suggested answers or completions. Select the one that BEST answers the question or completes the statement. *PRINT THE LETTER OF THE CORRECT ANSWER IN THE SPACE AT THE RIGHT.*

1. A commercial draft that specifies a payment date is termed

   A. line of credit
   B. sight draft
   C. time draft
   D. commercial paper

   1.____

2. The power to levy federal income tax is derived from the _____ Amendment to the Constitution.

   A. 2nd   B. 5th   C. 12th   D. 16th

   2.____

3. Which of the following steps in the process of new product development is concerned with the financial analysis of whether the product can make enough to justify the investment?

   A. Product testing
   B. Business analysis
   C. Segmentation
   D. Idea screening

   3.____

4. To determine the readability of a textual sample, which of the following should be done FIRST?

   A. Locating the point of intersection on a graph
   B. Counting the number of sentences in the sample
   C. Determining the appropriate grade level
   D. Counting the number of syllables in the sample

   4.____

5. A human-resources manager is directly responsible for each of the following EXCEPT

   A. supervision of the work force
   B. development of a productive work force
   C. maintenance of a satisfied work force
   D. acquisition of appropriate applicants

   5.____

6. An action whereby a court cancels a contract is known legally as

   A. disaffirmance
   B. rescission
   C. estoppel
   D. annulment

   6.____

7. To indirectly promote its product, a company uses an institutional aid to present its position on a social topic. This is an example of _____ advertising.

   A. cooperative
   B. brand
   C. advocacy
   D. generic

   7.____

8. A corporate code of ethics is a guide to acceptable and ethical behavior for relationships between a company and each of the following EXCEPT

   A. elected officials
   B. employees
   C. investors
   D. competitors

   8.____

9. What type of insurance policy covers costs for injury or death due to hazards at a place of business?

   A. Malpractice
   B. Public liability
   C. Whole life
   D. Product liability

10. On a typical memorandum, the identification line is typed

   A. indented, two lines beneath the reference line
   B. at the top of the page, just beneath the name and address
   C. flush or indented, directly beneath the subject line
   D. flush, two lines beneath the last line of the body or the signature initials, whichever is last

11. The most comprehensive business operated on foreign soil is a(n)

   A. franchise
   B. wholly owned subsidiary
   C. customs brokerage
   D. export trading company

12. *Goodwill* is considered to be a(n)

   A. fixed asset
   B. current asset
   C. intangible asset
   D. liability

13. When changed by the Federal Reserve, the discount rate is most likely to influence

   A. margin requirements
   B. the prime interest rate
   C. stock market gains
   D. reserve requirements

14. Business courses designed to deliver a curriculum for business are designed to help students develop occupational skills in business occupations. The two principal areas are the office occupations which facilitate business operations and the occupations which

   A. direct the distribution of goods and services
   B. rely to a small degree on interpersonal skills
   C. manage the status of untapped resources
   D. arrange for the financing of business operations

15. It is generally true that lower-income households

   A. are excluded from paying excise taxes
   B. spend a smaller proportion of their income on taxable products than do higher-income households
   C. spend a greater proportion of their income on taxable products
   D. spend about the same amount of their income on taxable products

16. An advantage associated with the use of commercial paper is that it

   A. can only be issued by blue-chip companies
   B. can be factored
   C. requires only a small compensating balance
   D. locks in an interest rate for up to a year

17. A typical business curriculum teaches that in the flow of an economy, government serves as each of the following EXCEPT

    A. transfer agent
    B. consumer
    C. manager
    D. producer

18. Sales processing, the handling of library loans, and airline reservation systems are examples of computerized _____ systems.

    A. executive information
    B. management information
    C. transaction processing
    D. decision support

19. Under the terms of the _____, a corporation must prepare a prospectus.

    A. Clayton Act of 1914
    B. Securities Act of 1933
    C. Securities and Exchange Act of 1934
    D. Federal Securities Act of 1964

20. The managers who oversee a business's production system are referred to as _____ managers.

    A. marketing
    B.
    C. operations
    D. financial

21. What is the term for a merger between firms in completely unrelated industries?

    A. Amalgamation
    B. Horizontal merger
    C. Vertical merger
    D. Conglomerate merger

22. The consumer attitude to buy before a price increase is likely to exist during periods of

    A. high inflation
    B. high unemployment
    C. low demand
    D. high employment

23. The process of transferring entries from journals to ledger accounts is known as

    A. double-entry
    B. posting
    C. closing
    D. cross-footing

24. What is the term for the development of a plan for production?

    A. Product design
    B. Design planning
    C. Planning table
    D. Process layout

25. On a standard typed sheet, or a suitable computer reproduction, how many line spaces equal one vertical inch?

    A. 2   B. 3   C. 6   D. 9

KEY (CORRECT ANSWERS)

1. C
2. D
3. B
4. B
5. A

6. B
7. C
8. A
9. B
10. D

11. B
12. C
13. B
14. A
15. C

16. D
17. C
18. C
19. B
20. C

21. D
22. A
23. B
24. B
25. C

TEST 2

DIRECTIONS: Each question or incomplete statement is followed by several suggested answers or completions. Select the one that BEST answers the question or completes the statement. *PRINT THE LETTER OF THE CORRECT ANSWER IN THE SPACE AT THE RIGHT.*

1. Preferred stock

    A. receives interest
    B. has a residual claim on assets
    C. represents ownership
    D. has voting rights

2. What type of computer system is likely to be used by designers, engineers, and other personnel who use applications such as computer-aided design (CAD)?

    A. Microcomputer
    B. Work station
    C. Mainframe
    D. Minicomputer

3. Each of the following is a feature of laissez-faire capitalism EXCEPT

    A. economic freedom
    B. competition
    C. private ownership of wealth
    D. guaranteed income

4. A factor will purchase accounts receivable for _____ value.

    A. their present
    B. more than their present
    C. less than their face
    D. their present

5. A *kinesthetic* learner will most likely _____ to recall information.

    A. write
    B. play back a recording
    C. speak
    D. visualize

6. _____ is another term for flexible manufacturing.

    A. Hard manufacturing
    B. Soft manufacturing
    C. Automation
    D. Variable manufacturing

7. Which of the following is not an IRS requirement for an automatic data processing system (ADM) used for business records? It must

    A. be electronically linked with the IRS computer processing system
    B. provide a way to trace any transaction back forward to the final total
    C. print out the general ledger and its source reference for the same period as the tax year
    D. provide an audit trail

8. A speculator would most likely invest in

    A. common stocks
    B. municipal bonds
    C. mutual funds
    D. Treasury bills

9. Which of the following is NOT an advantage associated with the use of a numerical filing system?

    A. Rapidity and accuracy of refiling
    B. Requirement of only one search for locating individual files
    C. Ability of data-processing systems to do more effective work
    D. Opportunity for indefinite expansion

10. Self-insurance is a practical method of risk

    A. reduction
    B. assumption
    C. transfer
    D. avoidance

11. Each of the following types of financing is usually appropriate for lifestyle businesses EXCEPT

    A. money from venture capitalists
    B. bank loans
    C. SBA loans
    D. personal savings or loans from friends

12. Economic theory states that society determines each of the following EXCEPT

    A. for whom goods and services will be produced
    B. how goods and services will be transported
    C. the quantity of goods and services to be produced
    D. how goods and services will be produced

13. Giving free samples of a product is an example of

    A. missionary selling
    B. sales promotion
    C. public relations
    D. advertising

14. A formal written instrument, such as a lease, that defines reciprocal rights and duties is called a(n)

    A. endorsement
    B. affirmation
    C. indenture
    D. contract

15. What type of insurance coverage MUST be offered by companies?

    A. Worker's compensation
    B. Major medical
    C. Life
    D. Dental and vision

16. What is the term for the processing of a group of documents at one time together as a unit?

    A. Lumping
    B. Merging
    C. Chunking
    D. Batching

17. When money retains its value over time, it is said to have

    A. stability
    B. portability
    C. durability
    D. divisibility

18. Generally, which of the following organizations or groups may NOT file for bankruptcy? 18.____

   A. Credit unions
   B. Partnerships
   C. Corporations
   D. Creditors

19. The value assigned for a business's reputation, calculated as the difference between the price paid for the business and the underlying value of its assets, is a characteristic known as 19.____

   A. goodwill
   B. margin
   C. return on investment
   D. equity

20. Which of the following is required under the legal principle of negotiability of instruments? 20.____

   A. An unspecified payee
   B. The instrument must be in writing
   C. A conditional promise to pay
   D. An open date for payment

21. In a unit on income, students are learning the principle that a person's income is closely related to the size, steadiness, and growth of the nation's income. The first thing students should do to develop an understanding of this principle would be to 21.____

   A. look through help-wanted ads in the local newspaper
   B. search for examples that illustrate how some family incomes may remain stable or decrease while a nation's Gross National Product (GNP) increases
   C. use flow analysis to develop an understanding of real income and money income
   D. develop a definition of GNP

22. As developed by mid-level managers, goals and plans covering a one-to-three year period to assist in obtaining broader companywide objectives are _____ in nature. 22.____

   A. operational
   B. strategic
   C. tactical
   D. programmed

23. The _____ Act declared monopolies to be illegal. 23.____

   A. Sherman Antitrust
   B. Robinson-Patman
   C. Clayton Antitrust
   D. Celler-Kefauver

24. Each of the following is a marketable security EXCEPT a 24.____

   A. chattel mortgage
   B. certificate of deposit
   C. Fannie Mae
   D. Treasury bill

25. Which of the following is considered to be advertising's MAIN advantage over other types of promotion? 25.____

   A. The Constitutional right to free speech
   B. Low-cost availability
   C. The compulsion of consumers to buy the organization's product
   D. Greatest control exercised by the organization

KEY (CORRECT ANSWERS)

1.	C		11.	A
2.	B		12.	B
3.	D		13.	B
4.	C		14.	C
5.	A		15.	A
6.	B		16.	D
7.	A		17.	A
8.	A		18.	A
9.	B		19.	A
10.	B		20.	B

21. D
22. C
23. A
24. A
25. D

TEST 3

DIRECTIONS: Each question or incomplete statement is followed by several suggested answers or completions. Select the one that BEST answers the question or completes the statement. *PRINT THE LETTER OF THE CORRECT ANSWER IN THE SPACE AT THE RIGHT.*

1. Which of the following statements about corporation bonds is TRUE? They

    A. pay dividends
    B. pay interest
    C. carry voting rights
    D. represent ownership

2. A _____ system is NOT a system commonly used for following up overdue accounts.

    A. tickler-card
    B. ledger
    C. punched-card
    D. multiple-invoice

3. An organization is most likely to use a direct distribution channel when

    A. there is little or no competition
    B. the product is relatively inexpensive
    C. customers are concentrated in a small geographic area
    D. each order is relatively small

4. Which of the following methods of visually displaying data tends to be most accurate?

    A. Column
    B. Graph
    C. Pie chart
    D. Bar chart

5. A company's taxes payable are considered to be _____ liabilities.

    A. intangible
    B. fixed
    C. long-term
    D. current

6. Consumer affairs offices such as the Better Business Bureau exist to fulfill the consumer's right to

    A. be heard
    B. be informed
    C. obtain credit
    D. safety

7. If a mutual fund is classified as *no-load*, its management fees are generally

    A. lower   B. higher   C. variable   D. waived

8. If a word-processing document needs to be permanently saved, what type of storage media should be used?

    A. Punched card
    B. RAM
    C. Magnetic
    D. ROM

9. Each of the following is a characteristic of public corporations EXCEPT

    A. the ability to raise large sums of money quickly
    B. limited liability
    C. limited life span
    D. ability to attract quality personnel

10. Which of the following basic understandings should be mastered FIRST by students during a unit on saving?

    A. Most people save with specific objectives in mind.
    B. Individuals and families often save as a result of fixed commitments.
    C. From the point of view of the economy as a whole, saving represents current income not spent for consumer goods and services.
    D. The amount of money saved by an individual or family may be influenced by certain variables.

11. Under the terms of _____, a company provides an injured worker with a partial income while he or she is injured and unable to work.

    A. employer income protection planning
    B. union income guarantee negotiations
    C. disability income insurance
    D. injured worker income guarantee plans

12. What is the term for a charge or claim against property that makes the property serve as security until some obligation is discharged?

    A. Garnishment   B. Lien
    C. Liquidation   D. Escrow

13. In union negotiations, which of the following would be an example of a permissive subject?

    A. Pension benefits   B. Health insurance for retirees
    C. Wages   D. Working hours

14. A small business may typically have each of the following advantages over a large business EXCEPT

    A. lower overhead
    B. quicker response to market changes
    C. stronger financial position
    D. provision of more specialized services

15. *Short-term* financing is money that is borrowed for a term of _____ or less.

    A. six months   B. one year
    C. two years   D. five years

16. Which of the following methods of inquiry is probably LEAST suitable for a personal economics curriculum?

    A. Opportunity cost   B. Freedom of choice
    C. Ratio analysis   D. Flow analysis

17. A wide span of management would probably be LEAST suitable for

    A. top-level managers
    B. managing a group of attorneys
    C. managing a group of neurosurgeons
    D. managing a group of production-line workers

18. Purchasing insurance is a method of risk

    A. reduction
    B. assumption
    C. transfer
    D. avoidance

19. Which of the following is a source of equity capital?

    A. Stockholders
    B. Bond holders
    C. Banks
    D. Insurance companies

20. The Customs Court is a(n)

    A. state court
    B. appellate court
    C. court of original jurisdiction
    D. court of limited jurisdiction

21. Which of the following is NOT an asset?

    A. Retained earnings
    B. Fixed
    C. Current
    D. Intangible

22. When a person is traveling to a foreign country on business, and funds of more than one thousand dollars are needed for the trip, which of the following travel fund arrangements will most likely be used?

    A. Traveler's checks
    B. Travel advance
    C. Letter of credit
    D. Personal checks

23. Examining market opportunities, allocating resources to capitalize those opportunities and predicting the success of these actions is a process known as

    A. strategic marketing planning
    B. target market definition
    C. market mix development
    D. market segmentation

24. During the presentation of a unit on investing, students should FIRST learn the principle that

    A. in choosing a personal investment, an individual should consider certain variables
    B. a business firm avoids the use of an intermediary when it uses its own savings to purchase additional capital goods
    C. some kinds of investments are generally considered safer than others, but all such investments contain an element of risk
    D. a stock exchange is an institution that aids in financial investment

25. Which of the following types of layout is illustrated by an automobile repair shop?

    A. Planning   B. Product   C. Process   D. Plant

KEY (CORRECT ANSWERS)

1.	B	11.	C
2.	C	12.	B
3.	C	13.	B
4.	B	14.	C
5.	D	15.	B
6.	A	16.	C
7.	B	17.	D
8.	C	18.	C
9.	C	19.	A
10.	C	20.	D

21. A
22. C
23. A
24. C
25. C

EXAMINATION SECTION
TEST 1

DIRECTIONS: Each question or incomplete statement is followed by several suggested answers or completions. Select the one that BEST answers the question or completes the statement. *PRINT THE LETTER OF THE CORRECT ANSWER IN THE SPACE AT THE RIGHT.*

1. When a check is written out of a company's checkbook, each of the following should also be entered on the check stub EXCEPT

   A. purpose of the payment
   B. transaction type
   C. amount
   D. payee

   1.____

2. An average markup is often used by businesses to

   A. maximize profits
   B. meet the competition on average
   C. avoid calculating the proper markup percentage for each of a large mix of products
   D. charge average prices in the marketplace

   2.____

3. Under the terms of business law, inventory is classified as

   A. an intangible asset
   B. intangible personal property
   C. tangible personal property
   D. real property

   3.____

4. What type of insurance policy provides protection against all forms of liability not specifically excluded under the terms of the policy?

   A. Comprehensive general liability
   B. Umbrella malpractice liability
   C. Comprehensive property
   D. Worker's compensation

   4.____

5. Which of the following is a demand deposit?

   A. Savings account
   B. Certificate of deposit
   C. Checking account
   D. Passbook account

   5.____

6. In initiating a social responsibility program, a business takes each of the following steps EXCEPT

   A. conducting a social audit
   B. development of a plan
   C. appointing a program director
   D. recognizing the existence of a problem

   6.____

7. Which of the following is NOT a step involved in production control?

   A. Routing
   B. Scheduling
   C. Handling
   D. Dispatching

   7.____

8. S-corporations must

    A. have several corporate stockholders
    B. own less than 80% of stock in another corporation
    C. have two classes of stock
    D. have more than 100 shareholders

9. Which of the following basic understandings should a student acquire EARLIEST in a unit on spending?

    A. Consumer spending helps to determine how much is produced.
    B. Consumer spending helps to determine whether individual businesses succeed or fail.
    C. Consumer spending helps to determine what goods and services are produced.
    D. Skill in spending can increase a consumer's effective purchasing power and raise his level of living.

10. The United States legislation that outlaws discrimination against buyers as well as sellers is the _____ Act.

    A. Antitrust Procedures and Penalties
    B. Celler-Kefauver
    C. Robinson-Patman
    D. Wheeler-Lea

11. Which of the following is a term for the act of totaling the columns in a book of accounts?

    A. Summation   B. Double-entering
    C. Capture   D. Cross-footing

12. A television ad for a Honda automobile is an example of _____ advertising.

    A. reminder   B. comparative
    C. immediate-response   D. selective

13. The resource used to convert raw materials into products is the _____ resource.

    A. financial   B. information
    C. material   D. human

14. If a company wants to have workers specialize in particular tasks and functions to bring about efficient production, the company should organize itself according to

    A. product   B. process   C. geography   D. customer

15. A linked network of computers that are wired to one another directly, instead of through telephone lines, is known as a(n)

    A. voice-mail system
    B. node-to-node system
    C. integrated voice-data system
    D. local area network (LAN)

16. Commercial paper is a _____ term promissory note issued in _____ denominations.

    A. short; small   B. long; large
    C. short; large   D. long; small

17. A business teacher wants to develop student understanding of the principle that the decisions of citizens and voters help to determine what goods and services are produced by an economy.
    Which of the following learning experiences would probably be LEAST helpful for the students' purposes?

    A. Determining what percentage of the United States' GNP consists of government expenditures
    B. Discussing the effects of government spending and taxation on economic growth and stability
    C. Listing examples of public wants that are satisfied through government action at various levels
    D. Obtaining examples of budgets for local, state, and federal governments

18. Which stage in the product life cycle involves the largest increase in sales AND the largest number of competitors?

    A. Introduction   B. Growth
    C. Maturity   D. Decline

19. Preferred stock dividends are

    A. specified on the stock market
    B. voted on by stockholders
    C. declared by the board of directors
    D. determined by top management

20. Which of the following is enforced by the Equal Employment Opportunity Commission (EEOC)?

    A. Occupational Safety and Health Act
    B. National Labor Relations Act
    C. Civil Rights Act
    D. Fair Labor Standards Act

21. Which of the following investments has the highest degree of safety?

    A. Certificate of deposit   B. Real estate
    C. Bonds   D. Stocks

22. In gathering data for its management information system, a company has used company records, reports, managers' meetings, and suppliers. How many of its information sources are *external* data sources?

    A. 1   B. 2   C. 3   D. 4

23. Which of the following types of production routing (layouts) would MOST likely be used in the construction of a building?

    A. Assembly-line   B. Service-line
    C. Process   D. Fixed-position

24. What is the term for the gradual reduction of a debt until it is extinguished by a series of periodic payments to a creditor? 24.____

   A. Accrual
   B. Decrement
   C. Amortization
   D. Subsidy

25. A _____ bond is secured by the assets of a corporation. 25.____

   A. convertible
   B. serial
   C. debenture
   D. mortgage

KEY (CORRECT ANSWERS)

1. B
2. C
3. C
4. A
5. C

6. D
7. C
8. B
9. D
10. C

11. D
12. A
13. D
14. B
15. B

16. C
17. C
18. B
19. A
20. C

21. A
22. A
23. D
24. C
25. D

TEST 2

DIRECTIONS: Each question or incomplete statement is followed by several suggested answers or completions. Select the one that BEST answers the question or completes the statement. *PRINT THE LETTER OF THE CORRECT ANSWER IN THE SPACE AT THE RIGHT.*

1. The purpose of specialization in the workplace is to

   A. increase the efficiency of workers
   B. reduce the training time of new employees
   C. boost the morale of workers
   D. relieve boredom

2. In negotiations, decisions made by a mediator are

   A. nonbinding to either party
   B. binding to the union
   C. binding to management
   D. binding to both management and the union

3. When company deposits are made at a bank, the checks are typically arranged in one of the following ways EXCEPT by

   A. the place where it is payable
   B. the name of the drawer
   C. check number
   D. transit number

4. Limits set by the Federal Reserve on the amount of money that stockbrokers and banks may lend customers for the purpose of buying stocks are known as

   A. selective credit controls
   B. investments caps
   C. margin requirements
   D. reserve requirements

5. In a unit on investment, a teacher wants to illustrate the principle that there is an immediate and continued effect on the economy when total savings are not placed in capital investments.
   Which of the following learning experiences would be MOST useful for this purpose?

   A. Illustrating the relationship of capital investment to economic stability and growth
   B. Interviewing an officer of a savings institution to find out what the institution does with its deposits
   C. Discussing the freedom of choice citizens have in influencing government investments
   D. Discussing the possible effect on financial institutions if there were a marked decrease in personal savings

6. Which of the following is an advantage associated with a general partnership?

   A. Ability to combine skills and knowledge
   B. Transferability of stock
   C. Frozen investments
   D. Unlimited liability

7. Identifying potential buyers, qualifying potential buyers, and generating sales leads are a part of the _____ stage in the creative selling process.

    A. preparing
    B. presenting
    C. approaching
    D. prospecting

8. How often do taxpayers who own sole proprietorships or partnerships pay income tax?

    A. Bimonthly
    B. Quarterly
    C. Semiannually
    D. Annually

9. For what reason do most small businesses fail?

    A. Inexperience
    B. Strict credit practices by lenders
    C. Slow growth in planned expansions
    D. Overextended credit

10. Which of the following is NOT a characteristic of the official letter style?

    A. Salutation placed 2-5 lines below the date line
    B. Open punctuation may be used in the address
    C. Identification line written 2 inches below the last line of the address
    D. First lines of paragraphs begin at extreme left

11. A _____ bond is a tax-free bond whose income is exempt from income taxes, and is backed by a city's taxing power.

    A. business development
    B. general obligation
    C. municipal
    D. revenue

12. In human resources management, which of the following is used in an objective appraisal evaluation method?

    A. Anecdotal observations
    B. Employee feedback
    C. Units of output
    D. Rating scales

13. As developed by top management, long-term goals and plans pertaining to broad, companywide issues are considered to be _____ in nature.

    A. tactical
    B. programmed
    C. strategic
    D. operational

14. What type of management information is needed by marketing managers?

    A. Pricing stragegies
    B. Inventory costs
    C. Personnel
    D. Interest rates

15. A(n) _____ tax is a tax that is assessed in the distribution channel on the difference between the cost of the good and the end price.

    A. excise
    B. value-added
    C. sales
    D. channel services

16. The MOST effective way of encouraging ethical business behavior is to

    A. pass government regulations
    B. establish a corporate code of ethics
    C. include ethics clauses in labor contracts
    D. provide guidelines from trade associations

17. What is the term for the situation that occurs when a manufacturer and middleman share advertising expenditures?

    A. Promotional campaign
    B. Institutional advertising
    C. Promotional mix
    D. Cooperative advertising

18. Which of the following is a term for taking or seizing a debtor's property to place it under the control of a court?

    A. Abrogation
    B. Garnishment
    C. Attachment
    D. Debenture

19. _____ is the term for the act of rewarding workers with dollar bonuses given according to team effort in areas that employees can directly influence.

    A. Gain sharing
    B. Employee stock option
    C. Empowerment
    D. Employee-owned business

20. Which of the following industries does NOT involve a regulated monopoly?

    A. Communications
    B. Transportation
    C. Steel
    D. Public utilities

21. What type of skills are represented by the ability to identify the relevant issues in a situation in order to determine how they are related?

    A. Technical
    B. Analytic
    C. Conceptual
    D. Diagnostic

22. In a contract, the words *without recourse* are followed by the payee's _____ endorsement.

    A. qualified
    B. restrictive
    C. blank
    D. special

23. A company that wants to serve the mass market is following the _____ approach to market segmentation.

    A. concentrated
    B. customized
    C. undifferentiated
    D. differentiated

24. A contract that calls for immediate delivery of a set amount of grain is termed a

    A. commodity swap
    B. futures trade
    C. money-market-managed investment
    D. spot trade

25. A commercial draft is generally issued when the

    A. supplier must generate funds for short-term credit
    B. supplier has reservations about the customer's credit
    C. supplier has good credit
    D. federal government needs to raise funds

KEY (CORRECT ANSWERS)

1. A
2. B
3. C
4. C
5. D
6. A
7. D
8. B
9. A
10. D

11. B
12. C
13. C
14. A
15. B
16. B
17. C
18. C
19. A
20. C

21. B
22. A
23. C
24. D
25. B

TEST 3

DIRECTIONS: Each question or incomplete statement is followed by several suggested answers or completions. Select the one that BEST answers the question or completes the statement. *PRINT THE LETTER OF THE CORRECT ANSWER IN THE SPACE AT THE RIGHT.*

1. On an organization chart, solid vertical lines indicate relationships between

    A. management and staff positions
    B. line positions
    C. all employees
    D. staff positions

    1.____

2. Depositors are penalized for early withdrawals of funds from

    A. certificates of deposit   B. lines of credit
    C. notes payable   D. NOW accounts

    2.____

3. What is the term for salespeople who are responsible for building relationships with wholesalers and retailers by setting up displays and giving in-store demonstrations?

    A. Order takers   B. Missionary salespeople
    C. Trade salespeople   D. Technical salespeople

    3.____

4. In a unit on income, students should FIRST learn the principle that

    A. an individual's real income is the amount of goods and services that can be bought with the money she receives
    B. money is a social invention designed to direct and facilitate the flow of goods and services
    C. an individual may increase his income earning ability by improving his knowledge or skill and by making a wise choice of occupation
    D. an individual's income is usually closely related to the size, steadiness, and growth of the nation's income

    4.____

5. Which of the following steps in the operational planning process would be performed first?
    The

    A. comparison of demand with capacity
    B. adjustment of output to match demand
    C. selection of a planning horizon
    D. estimation of market demand

    5.____

6. Under the Trade Expansion Act, the authority to negotiate reciprocal trade agreements that could reduce United States tariffs was granted for a period of _____ years.

    A. 2   B. 5   C. 10   D. 30

    6.____

7. Currently, protectionist pressures are increasing in the United States because

    A. many see foreign competition as causing a loss of employment in the United States
    B. trade barriers cost United States consumers approximately $60 million a year
    C. many want to make a statement of support for United States industry
    D. protectionism typically leads to retaliation

    7.____

73

8. Most government regulation of business involves

   A. corporations
   B. sole proprietorships
   C. cooperatives
   D. partnerships

9. Which of the following is a statement of the matching principle?

   A. Capital investments should equal long-term debt.
   B. The timing of borrowing should equal the timing of spending.
   C. A firm's debt should equal its equity.
   D. Leverage should equal short-term debt.

10. When a company's petty cash fund is getting low, or at the end of a specified period, which of the following documents is usually prepared and submitted?

    A. Balance sheet
    B. General journal
    C. Debenture
    D. Record of transactions

11. The _____ Act declared interlocking directories to be illegal.

    A. Sherman Antitrust
    B. Robinson-Patman
    C. Clayton Antitrust
    D. Federal Trade Commission

12. What is the term for the process of breaking raw materials into one or more distinct products?

    A. Synthetic system
    B. Distillation
    C. Flexible manufacturing
    D. Analytic system

13. A written document issued and signed by one party, requiring the addressee to pay a specified amount to a third party, is a(n)

    A. bill of exchange
    B. bank draft
    C. writ of attachment
    D. sight draft

14. What is the term for insurance in which one party agrees to be responsible to a second party for the obligations of a third party?

    A. Surety bond
    B. Fidelity bond
    C. Nonperformance contract
    D. Credit life

15. A teacher is preparing a unit on making economic decisions as a citizen. Which of the following principles would most likely be taught *earliest* in the unit?

    A. The decisions that individuals make as citizens or voters help to determine what goods and services are produced.
    B. Decisions that individual citizens make today will help to determine the future role of private enterprise and government in the economy.
    C. To maintain economic freedom, people have the responsibility to make wise decisions.
    D. Some wants of individuals can best be satisfied for the public through government action.

16. Which of the following is a method of internal recruiting?

    A. Private agencies
    B. Union hiring
    C. Job posting
    D. Newspaper advertisements

17. Organizational products that involve large outlays of capital, and that are major pieces of equipment and/or buildings used to make other products, are termed

    A. components
    B. installations
    C. supplies
    D. fixtures

18. The most common method of resolving labor-management disputes is by

    A. injunction
    B. employment of strikebreakers
    C. strike
    D. collective bargaining

19. Which of the following learning experiences would be most effective in developing students' understanding that most people save with specific objectives in mind?

    A. Using flow analysis to determine what would happen if savings of individuals and businesses were not used to purchase additional producer goods
    B. Preparing a list of the variables they feel influence the amount an individual or business saves
    C. Comparing the use of credit with saving
    D. Discussing how opportunity cost is involved in saving

20. The Equal Employment Opportunity Commission's regulations fall under the provisions of _____ law.

    A. statutory
    B. civil
    C. common
    D. administrative

21. What is the term for an IOU issued by a corporation to raise short-term capital?

    A. Debenture
    B. Commercial paper
    C. Certificate of deposit
    D. Thrift

22. What is the term for the things an individual or business must do without when a particular allocation of productive resources is decided upon?

    A. Freedom of choice
    B. Stricture
    C. Opportunity cost
    D. Gap analysis

23. Which of the following is NOT a disadvantage commonly associated with sole proprietorship?

    A. The tendency to be small-scale in size and profit
    B. Unlimited liability
    C. The high interest rates encountered by owners borrowing money
    D. The difficulty most people have in establishing the proprietorship

24. What type of computer command enables a user to print two or more documents from a single display?

    A. Merge   B. Link   C. Help   D. Insert

25. Bond prices are quoted in the form of

    A. dollars
    B. percentages
    C. yield
    D. points

KEY (CORRECT ANSWERS)

1.	B	11.	C
2.	A	12.	D
3.	C	13.	A
4.	B	14.	A
5.	C	15.	D
6.	B	16.	C
7.	A	17.	B
8.	A	18.	D
9.	B	19.	D
10.	D	20.	D
21.	B		
22.	C		
23.	D		
24.	A		
25.	B		

EXAMINATION SECTION
TEST 1

DIRECTIONS: Each question or incomplete statement is followed by several suggested answers or completions. Select the one that BEST answers the question or completes the statement. *PRINT THE LETTER OF THE CORRECT ANSWER IN THE SPACE AT THE RIGHT.*

1. In production and operations control, choosing the site of the production facility is a function of the _____ process. 1.____

    A. production design
    B. selection
    C. production planning
    D. production evaluation

2. Each of the following is an advantage associated with high job specialization EXCEPT for 2.____

    A. facilitating scientific method study
    B. saving time in switching from one task to another
    C. being well–suited to small, entrepreneurial companies
    D. increasing worker dexterity

3. A statement of the duties, working conditions, and other significant requirements associated with a particular job is termed a 3.____

    A. replacement chart
    B. job specification
    C. job description
    D. job analysis

4. A _____ organizational plan is illustrated by a company's method for figuring overtime pay. 4.____

    A. short–term
    B. long–term
    C. single–use
    D. standing

5. Which of the following files lists the names and quantities of all items that are required to produce one unit of product? 5.____

    A. Inventory
    B. Output
    C. MRP
    D. Bill of materials

6. Which of the following is NOT a branch of the quantitative management approach? 6.____

    A. Behavioral science
    B. Management information systems
    C. Operations management
    D. Management science

7. During a staff development meeting, several employees are asked to view some videotapes that illustrate a process related to job performance, and are then asked to tape and observe their own performance of this activity.
This is an example of 7.____

    A. understudy
    B. socialization
    C. behavior modeling
    D. apprenticeship

8. _____ is a statistical technique that involves evaluating random samples from a group of produced materials to determine whether the group meets agreeable quality levels.

   A. Statistical process control
   B. Acceptance sampling
   C. Raw materials sampling
   D. AQL

9. A formal business group, consisting of a manager and all the subordinates who report to that manager, is known as a(n)

   A. strategic business unit
   B. reference group
   C. command group
   D. module

10. Which of the following ideas was contributed by the classical viewpoint of management?

    A. The visualization of organizations as systems of interrelated parts
    B. The managerial importance of leadership
    C. There is no one best way to manage
    D. The importance of pay as a motivator

11. Each of the following is a component of quality control EXCEPT

    A. marketability
    B. function
    C. aesthetics
    D. safety

12. The human resource needs of a company are determined *primarily* by

    A. a human resource audit
    B. the company's goals and strategies
    C. the legal environment
    D. a replacement chart

13. If an employee is terminated as a result of _____, this is an example of *due cause*.

    A. layoff
    B. incompetence
    C. retirement
    D. plant closing

14. According to the systems approach to management, there are four major components to an organizational system. Which of the following is NOT one of these components?

    A. Inputs
    B. Transformation processes
    C. Feedback
    D. Raw materials

15. Tactical problems are *primarily* the responsibility of

    A. workers
    B. low-level managers
    C. middle-level managers
    D. executives

16. Robert Owens' (1771–1858) contribution to management theory involved

    A. human resources
    B. cognitive theory
    C. work specialization
    D. behaviorist theory

17. The _____ dimension of quality involves the degree to which a product's design or operating characteristics meet established standards.

    A. reliability
    B. conformance
    C. serviceability
    D. durability

18. Which type of technology is illustrated by a commercial bank?

    A. Long–linked
    B. Intensive
    C. Long–term
    D. Mediating

19. According to situational leadership theory, the technique of *telling* is used when followers are

    A. able to take responsibility but are unwilling or too insecure to do so
    B. able and willing to take responsibility
    C. unable to take responsibility but are willing to do so
    D. unable and unwilling or too insecure to take responsibility for a given task

20. The principles of management by objectives (MBO) include each of the following EXCEPT

    A. executive–proposed goals
    B. managerial–subordinate discussion
    C. mutual goal–setting
    D. performance feedback

21. Each of the following is considered to be a valuable characteristic of layout design EXCEPT

    A. reduction of material transport cost, but not time
    B. bottleneck–free floor design
    C. employee safety provisions
    D. minimizing travel distance required for worker to reach materials

22. What stage of group development deals with accomplishing assigned tasks?

    A. Internal problem–solving
    B. Growth and productivity
    C. Orientation
    D. Evaluation and control

23. Typically, which of the following steps in the budgetary process would occur FIRST?

    A. Unit manager formulation of unit's operating plans
    B. Top management outlines resource restraints
    C. Top management combines information
    D. Unit managers determine resource needs

24. In a matching analysis, what has occurred when an external opportunity matches the internal strength of a company?

    A. Problem
    B. Vulnerability
    C. Leverage
    D. Constraint

25. What type of reinforcement schedule is illustrated by a weekly paycheck?

    A. Variable interval
    B. Variable ratio
    C. Fixed interval
    D. Fixed ratio

24._____

25._____

KEY (CORRECT ANSWERS)

1. B
2. C
3. C
4. D
5. D

6. A
7. C
8. B
9. C
10. D

11. A
12. B
13. B
14. D
15. C

16. A
17. B
18. D
19. D
20. A

21. A
22. B
23. B
24. C
25. C

TEST 2

DIRECTIONS: Each question or incomplete statement is followed by several suggested answers or completions. Select the one that BEST answers the question or completes the statement. *PRINT THE LETTER OF THE CORRECT ANSWER IN THE SPACE AT THE RIGHT.*

1. A management approach that is oblivious to ethical considerations is described as   1.____

   A. unethical   B. amoral   C. libertine   D. immoral

2. Informal leaders could serve a valuable role in a company when   2.____

   A. they defer to organizational power
   B. their influence is compatible with the company's goals
   C. they make other people feel satisfied with their own performance
   D. their activity receives praise from higher management

3. Moving from marketing to production is an example of a(n) _____ of career path.   3.____

   A. vertical   B. circumferential
   C. radial   D. cone

4. Each of the following is a DISADVANTAGE associated with the use of a rational model for decision–making in a company EXCEPT   4.____

   A. preferences cannot be ranked in a permanent way
   B. payoffs are difficult to estimate
   C. not all necessary information is available
   D. environmental conditions cannot be accurately forecast

5. The MAIN advantage to product departmentalization is   5.____

   A. duplication of efforts
   B. adaptability
   C. achieving economies of scale
   D. innovation

6. The decision to hire a new employee is a(n) _____ decision.   6.____

   A. programmed   B. nonprogrammed
   C. detail   D. under certainty

7. Which of the following are concerned with departmental or interdepartmental activities?   7.____

   A. Policies   B. Procedures
   C. Rules   D. Goals and strategies

8. Each of the following is a legal concern associated with job testing EXCEPT   8.____

   A. length of the test
   B. reliability of the test
   C. relation of test to the job
   D. whether test measures what it professes to measure

9. The settling of disputes over contract language during collective bargaining is known as _____ arbitration.   9.____

   A. interest   B. verbal   C. rights   D. contract

10. In an oligopolistic economic environment, there are _____ sellers and _____ buyers.

    A. many; few
    B. many; many
    C. few; many
    D. few; few

11. What term would be used to describe a company whose decision-making power is dispersed among lower-level managers?

    A. Thin
    B. Decentralized
    C. Flat
    D. Fat

12. The effort to solve problems by beginning with a problem and attempting to move logically to a solution is known as

    A. the rational model
    B. convergent thinking
    C. the incremental model
    D. divergent thinking

13. If a manager determines that controls are needed but the control process will be too costly, each of the following is an alternative to controls EXCEPT

    A. changing the dependence relationship
    B. implementing horizontal integration
    C. changing organizational goals and objectives to eliminate dependence
    D. changing the nature of the dependence

14. Each of the following is an advantage associated with the use of internal recruitment in the management of human resources EXCEPT

    A. availability of reliable candidate information
    B. rewarding of good performance
    C. increased internal morale due to upward mobility opportunities
    D. increased likelihood of new ideas being introduced

15. A company uses an organizational design in which a product structure overlays a functional structure. What type of design structure is being used?

    A. Functional
    B. Matrix
    C. Contingency
    D. Classical

16. The allocation of a company's financial resources is known as the _____ process.

    A. capital development
    B. financial evaluation
    C. budgeting
    D. equity sourcing

17. Developing plans, setting goals, and making decisions are part of

    A. coordination
    B. influencing
    C. formulation
    D. implementation

18. Generally, the consumerism movement is concerned with each of the following EXCEPT

    A. price fixing
    B. retail complaint-handling
    C. equal opportunity employment
    D. deceptive labeling

19. A company's management sets a goal of achieving a 12% return on investment capital from the sale of a company's product line. What type of goal has the company set?

    A. Operative
    B. Official
    C. Operational
    D. Short–term

19.____

20. When a company's turnover rate is too low,

    A. replacement costs are too high
    B. there has been blocking of lower–level personnel
    C. insufficient weeding out has taken place
    D. a shortage of capable managers exists

20.____

21. A ratio that compares the owner's financial contributions to a company with creditors' contributions is called the _____ ratio.

    A. leverage
    B. profitability
    C. liquidity
    D. operating

21.____

22. The production evaluation process is primarily concerned with _____ control.

    A. input   B. output   C. marginal   D. process

22.____

23. _____ is considered a structural barrier to managerial automation.

    A. Incompatible systems
    B. Uncertainty avoidance
    C. Resistance
    D. A reward system that emphasizes quick and dramatic results

23.____

24. After an affirmative action plan has been written by a reporting company, a copy is required to be forwarded to the

    A. Department of Labor
    B. Equal Employment Opportunity Commission (EEOC)
    C. National Labor Relations Board
    D. Department of Human Service

24.____

25. Historically, the management theory that first focused on principles that could be used by managers to coordinate the internal activities of organizations was the theory of _____ management.

    A. behaviorist
    B. quantitative
    C. administrative
    D. bureaucratic

25.____

KEY (CORRECT ANSWERS)

1. B
2. B
3. B
4. C
5. B

6. A
7. B
8. A
9. A
10. C

11. B
12. B
13. B
14. D
15. B

16. C
17. C
18. C
19. A
20. C

21. A
22. B
23. D
24. A
25. C

TEST 3

DIRECTIONS: Each question or incomplete statement is followed by several suggested answers or completions. Select the one that BEST answers the question or completes the statement. *PRINT THE LETTER OF THE CORRECT ANSWER IN THE SPACE AT THE RIGHT.*

1. Which of the following is a financial resource for a company? 1.____

    A. Raw material reserves B. Reputation for quality
    C. Bond issues D. Warehouses

2. Discretionary expense centers are LEAST likely to be used with _____ departments. 2.____

    A. finance
    B. human resources
    C. research and development
    D. public relations

3. _____ managerial power is said to come from the individual, rather than from the company. 3.____

    A. Coercive B. Reward
    C. Expert D. Legitimate

4. The data inputs to computer-based executive support-systems are probably 4.____

    A. transactions B. aggregate data
    C. high-volume data D. analytic models

5. What type of audit involves the evaluation and assessment of an entire company's operations? 5.____

    A. Management B. Social
    C. External D. Internal

6. Performance feedback that is NOT evaluative is described as 6.____

    A. informal B. reinforcing
    C. dispersed D. informational

7. Which type of leader power stems from a position's placement in the managerial hierarchy and the authority vested in the position? 7.____

    A. Legitimate B. Referent
    C. Expert D. Reward

8. In matrix organizations, the BEST strategy for conflict resolution is typically 8.____

    A. conciliation B. consensus
    C. confrontation D. aversion

9. Which of the following is a destructive force that is MOST likely to affect the implementation phase of the development of a quality circle? 9.____

    A. Disagreement on problems
    B. Raised aspirations
    C. Prohibitive costs
    D. Burnout

10. An accountant who audits a company's books would use the _____ style of decision-making.

    A. intuitive
    B. systematic
    C. compensatory
    D. preceptive

11. Which functional area of a company involves equity ratio?

    A. Finance
    B. Marketing
    C. Operations
    D. Development

12. A company's plan for the acquisition or divestiture of major fixed assets is the

    A. profit budget
    B. balance sheet
    C. expense budget
    D. capital expenditures budget

13. The main DISADVANTAGE associated with job simplification is

    A. higher training costs
    B. lack of quality control mechanism
    C. lowered employee motivation
    D. loss of production efficiency

14. A company uses a compensation system in which employees throughout the organization are encouraged to become involved in solving problems, and are given bonuses tied to organizational performance improvements.
    This is an example of

    A. skill-based pay
    B. gainsharing
    C. benchmarking
    D. expanded commission

15. A task force formed by a company is responsible to

    A. the local community
    B. top-level management
    C. union leaders
    D. stockholders

16. What is the term for the identification of a trend and smoothing its pattern?

    A. Segmentation
    B. Moving average
    C. Time-series analysis
    D. Replacement analysis

17. _____ is a term for grouping jobs horizontally.

    A. Aggregation
    B. Departmentalization
    C. Formalization
    D. Dispersion

18. Which type of power, if exercised by a manager, is MOST likely to result in resistance by subordinates?

    A. Reward   B. Expert   C. Coercive   D. Referent

19. In manufacturing, MRP systems use three major inputs. Which of the following is NOT one of these three?

    A. Bill of materials information
    B. Investment information
    C. Inventory status information
    D. Master production schedule

20. What type of quality control is concerned *primarily* with the quality of raw input materials?

    A. Output
    B. Feed–forward
    C. Feedback
    D. Work in process

21. When groups are slow to reach a decision, they are demonstrating

    A. assembly effect
    B. entropy
    C. process loss
    D. synergy

22. _____ costs are those associated with acquiring raw materials.

    A. Storage
    B. Contingency
    C. Order
    D. Carrying

23. An effective managerial control system is each of the following EXCEPT

    A. focused
    B. flexible
    C. future–oriented
    D. timely

24. During what stage of orientation does an employee acquire technical skills that are likely to improve her current job performance?

    A. Induction
    B. Implementation
    C. Socialization
    D. Training

25. In a bureaucracy, the practice of adding unnecessary subordinates is likely to create

    A. red tape
    B. position protection
    C. dominance of authority
    D. inflexibility

KEY (CORRECT ANSWERS)

1. C
2. A
3. C
4. B
5. A
6. D
7. A
8. C
9. C
10. B
11. A
12. D
13. C
14. B
15. B
16. C
17. B
18. C
19. B
20. B
21. C
22. C
23. A
24. D
25. C

EXAMINATION SECTION
TEST 1

DIRECTIONS: Each question or incomplete statement is followed by several suggested answers or completions. Select the one that BEST answers the question or completes the statement. *PRINT THE LETTER OF THE CORRECT ANSWER IN THE SPACE AT THE RIGHT.*

1. An individual incentive plan where pay fluctuates based on units of production per time period is described as

    A. red circle
    B. standard-hour
    C. differential piece rate
    D. straight piecework

    1.____

2. In the experience of most employees, which of the following career stages lasts approximately from age 30 to 45?

    A. Midcareer crisis
    B. Advancement
    C. Maintenance
    D. Establishment

    2.____

3. Which of the following statements about effective leadership is generally NOT accepted by human resource managers?

    A. Employees often expect a supervisor to structure their behavior.
    B. A combination of high-supportive and high-directive styles is often a successful leadership style.
    C. Higher management will often set preferences regarding the leadership styles of lower-level managers and supervisors.
    D. Under emergency or high-pressure situations, emphasis on personal well-being is desirable and often preferred by employees.

    3.____

4. The Employment Retirement Income Security Act (ERISA), as amended, limits the eligibility requirements that an employer may establish for receiving retirement benefits. Specifically, an employer is prohibited from establishing a requirement of more than _____ of service.

    A. six months
    B. one year
    C. 3 years
    D. 5 years

    4.____

5. In a company's compensation policy, the most significant factor determining the company's external competitiveness is/are its

    A. benefits
    B. mix of various forms of pay
    C. career opportunities
    D. level of pay

    5.____

6. In an organization with a human resources department, which of the following information is most likely to be covered by the human resources manager in orienting a new employee?

    A. Introducing the new employee to other employees in the work unit
    B. Communicating the objectives and philosophy of the organization

    6.____

C. Discussing policies on performance and conduct
D. Familiarizing the employee with the physical work environment

7. The Age Discrimination in Employment Act of 1968 prohibits discrimination against individuals who are over _____ years of age.

   A. 30 B. 40 C. 50 D. 60

8. Which of the following types of personnel are most likely to be recruited with the assistance of private employment agencies?

   A. Commissioned sales
   B. Office/clerical
   C. Production/service
   D. Managers/supervisors

9. Advocates of hierarchical pay structures believe

   A. equal treatment will result in more knowledgeable employees going unrewarded and unrecognized
   B. all employees in an organization have an equal number of compensable factors
   C. managers should by virtue of their position earn more than line workers
   D. seniority should be the primary factor on which pay is based

10. In designing a training program for employees, it is important to remember that usually the first stage of learning is described as

    A. behavioral
    B. cognitive
    C. performance alteration
    D. experimental

11. In a(n) _____ situation, all employees pay union dues whether or not they are union members.

    A. decertified
    B. agency shop
    C. craft union
    D. collective bargaining

12. In the employee training process, which of the following tasks is most likely to be jointly undertaken by both the human resources manager and the operating manager?

    A. Selecting the trainer
    B. Developing training criteria
    C. Doing the training
    D. Evaluating the training

13. In behavioral theory, a decline in the rate of a behavior that is brought about by nonreinforcement is known as

    A. extinction
    B. norming
    C. regression
    D. conformity

14. Of all the relationships between performance evaluation and other personnel management activities, the most critical to understand today is the relationship between evaluation and

    A. human resources research
    B. equal employment opportunity
    C. motivation
    D. productivity

15. The main disadvantage of the *hot stove* method of employee discipline is that 15.____

    A. its benefits are more long-term than immediate
    B. it fails to recognize individual and situational differences
    C. it invites personal bias on the part of the manager
    D. does not allow for detailed recordkeeping

16. Today, the average employer can be expected to pay about _____ a year or more per employee for benefits. 16.____

    A. $1,000   B. $5,000   C. $9,000   D. $12,000

17. Supervised training and testing for a minimum time period, until an employee has acquired a minimum skill level, is commonly referred to as 17.____

    A. apprenticeship training   B. vestibule training
    C. on-the-job training   D. programmed instruction

18. Most human resource professionals believe that the most effective approach to on-the-job training for managers involves 18.____

    A. a mix of transfers (to new geographic locations) and rotations through jobs
    B. mentoring
    C. vestibule training
    D. coaching and counseling, coupled with a structured rotation through jobs and functions

19. The motivation-maintenance theory of employee management deals primarily with motivation through 19.____

    A. job design   B. collegiality
    C. behavioral modification   D. external rewards

20. In what year did the American Federation of Labor (AFL) merge with the Congress of Industrial Organizations (CIO)? 20.____

    A. 1886   B. 1938   C. 1955   D. 1966

21. Which of the following is a *critical-incident* system for rating employees? 21.____

    A. Alteration ranking
    B. Behavioral observation scale (BOS)
    C. Classification
    D. Forced-choice rating

22. Likely pitfalls to management by objectives (MBO) include each of the following EXCEPT 22.____

    A. too much emphasis on the long term
    B. failure to tie MBO results with rewards
    C. too much paperwork
    D. setting too many objectives

23. Typically, organizations that implement group incentive programs are most likely to use _____ as the basis for group pay.

    A. customer satisfaction
    B. quality
    C. financial measures
    D. productivity measures (output to input ratios)

24. Which of the following skills is most likely to be taught in training programs at a U.S. organization?

    A. Computer skills
    B. Clerical skills
    C. Executive development
    D. Customer relations

25. If an employer is found guilty, upon inspection by OSHA, of a serious violation of the federal health and safety code, and it is found that the violation is negligent rather than willful, the penalty is typically

    A. $1,000 per citation
    B. $10,000 per citation
    C. $10,000 or up to six months in jail
    D. $10,000 and/or six months in jail

KEY (CORRECT ANSWERS)

1.	D	11.	B
2.	B	12.	A
3.	D	13.	A
4.	B	14.	B
5.	D	15.	B
6.	B	16.	C
7.	B	17.	A
8.	D	18.	D
9.	A	19.	A
10.	B	20.	C

21. B
22. A
23. C
24. A
25. A

TEST 2

DIRECTIONS: Each question or incomplete statement is followed by several suggested answers or completions. Select the one that BEST answers the question or completes the statement. *PRINT THE LETTER OF THE CORRECT ANSWER IN THE SPACE AT THE RIGHT.*

1. Which of the following statements about employment agencies and executive search firms is/are TRUE? 1.____
     I. Most employment agencies work on retainer.
     II. Executive agencies are paid only when they have actually provided a new hire.
     III. Executive search firms generally do a better job of maintaining confidentiality.
   The CORRECT answer is:

   A. I only   B. I, II   C. III only   D. I, II, III

2. _____ is a training method in which, after material is presented in text form, a trainee is required to read and answer questions relating to the text. 2.____

   A. Cross-training
   B. Programmed instruction
   C. Apprenticeship training
   D. Classroom training

3. In the training process, which of the following is most likely to be done by the operating manager? 3.____

   A. Doing the training
   B. Developing training criteria
   C. Determining training needs and objectives
   D. Developing training material

4. The purpose of a market pay line is to 4.____

   A. pull the wages of competitors upward
   B. determine the maximum total payroll needed to maintain profit and productivity
   C. discourage the formation of a labor union
   D. summarize the pay rates of various jobs in the labor market

5. When selection procedures at an organization involve the use of tests to measure leadership characteristics and/or personality, tests with _____ validity are generally most appropriate. 5.____

   A. construct
   B. content
   C. alternate-form
   D. criterion-related

6. Which of the following is NOT a typical disadvantage associated with variable pay plans? Employees 6.____

   A. are unable to minimize risk through diversification
   B. may be likely to intentionally decrease their individual effort
   C. tend to count on bonus pay regardless of the likelihood of receiving it
   D. may feel penalized for factors beyond their control

7. Which of the following is an employee rating method, using 6 to 10 performance dimensions, that uses critical incidents as anchor statements placed along a scale?

    A. Forced-choice rating
    B. Behaviorally anchored rating scale (BARS)
    C. Forced-distribution rating
    D. Behavioral observation scale (BOS)

8. Many organizations today provide an alternative to traditional career pathing, and base career paths on real-world experiences and individualized preferences. Paths of this kind typically have each of the following characteristics EXCEPT

    A. they are definite and remain stable when organizational needs change
    B. they include lateral and downward possibilities
    C. each job along the path is specified in terms of acquirable skills and knowledge rather than merely educational credentials or work experience
    D. they are flexible enough to take individual qualities into account

9. Title VI of the 1964 Civil Rights Act prohibits discrimination based on several characteristics in all programs or activities that receive federal financial aid in order to provide employment. Which of the following types of discrimination is NOT explicitly outlawed by this law?

    A. Race
    B. Sex
    C. Color
    D. National origin

10. Which of the following types of organizations is exempt from the provisions of the Occupational Safety and Health Act?

    A. Businesses employing 15 or fewer people
    B. Government contractors for projects whose costs total less than $50,000
    C. Businesses employing only family members
    D. Businesses in non-industrial service sectors

11. Which of the following is not a legally mandated employee benefit?

    A. Family leave
    B. Unemployment compensation
    C. Worker's compensation
    D. Child care

12. Human resource planning is LEAST likely to be important if the goals of top management include

    A. rapid expansion
    B. merging
    C. stable growth
    D. diversification

13. _____ is the process of grouping personnel activities into related work units.

    A. Apportionment
    B. Allotment
    C. Blocking
    D. Departmentation

14. Of the following criteria used in the selection process, which is most potentially troublesome in light of equal employment opportunity laws? 14.____

    A. Personal characteristics
    B. Physical characteristics
    C. Experience/past performance
    D. Formal education

15. Each of the following is generally true of a laissez-faire leader and the group in his or her charge EXCEPT 15.____

    A. decisions are typically made by whoever is willing to make them
    B. morale is low
    C. individuals have little interest in their work
    D. the leader is very conscious of his or her position

16. A work situation in which a union is not present and there is no management effort to keep a union out is known as a(n) _____ shop. 16.____

    A. preferential   B. open
    C. restricted   D. closed

17. In a job evaluation that is conducted using the point method, which of the following would typically be performed FIRST? 17.____

    A. Preparing job descriptions
    B. Choosing compensable factors
    C. Establishing factor scales
    D. Conducting job analysis

18. The Pregnancy Discrimination Act requires employers to 18.____

    A. allow up to twelve weeks of leave for birth or adoption
    B. ask job candidates whether they are pregnant
    C. not consider pregnancy to be a disability
    D. treat pregnancy just like any other medical condition with regard to fringe benefits and leave policies

19. An agreement between an employee and management, that, as a condition of employment, the employee will not join a labor union, is known as a _____ contract. 19.____

    A. wildcat   B. zero-tolerance
    C. yellow-dog   D. submission

20. Effective human resource departments distinguish between employee training as an ongoing activity and training as a strategic tool for attaining the goals of the organization and the employees. In general, training for specific, measurable impact is characterized by a 20.____

    A. programmed sequence based on existing programs
    B. training environment that is separate from the work environment
    C. partnership with the client
    D. link to a philosophy rather than a business need

21. Which of the following statements about comparable worth is FALSE? It

    A. is the principal method suggested to reduce the earnings gap between men and women
    B. provides a plan for racial equity in the labor market
    C. allows external market concerns to dominate internal equity
    D. focuses on pay differences among different occupations

22. The use of employee referrals is sometimes a powerful personnel recruitment technique, but it has the important potential disadvantage of

    A. fostering jealousy and resentment among employees
    B. taking some decision-making powers away from management
    C. discouraging a shared sense of responsibility
    D. risking accidental violation of equal employment opportunity laws

23. When labor and management are in conflict on an issue, and when the outcome is a win/lose situation, _____ is said to be occurring.

    A. distributive bargaining   B. forced-choice ranking
    C. integrative bargaining   D. collective bargaining

24. Human resource managers sometimes deal with employee surpluses by encouraging attrition. The main potential disadvantage associated with this approach is that it

    A. involves costly severance packages
    B. can amount to layoffs of older employees
    C. occurs too slowly to be considered responsive to current surpluses
    D. discourages new ideas and experimentation from younger employees

25. In which of the following industries is the highest percentage of workers represented by unions?

    A. Manufacturing   B. Construction
    C. Wholesale/retail trade   D. Government workers

KEY (CORRECT ANSWERS)

1. C
2. B
3. A
4. D
5. A

6. B
7. B
8. A
9. B
10. C

11. D
12. C
13. D
14. B
15. D

16. B
17. D
18. D
19. C
20. C

21. C
22. D
23. A
24. B
25. D

EXAMINATION SECTION
TEST 1

DIRECTIONS: Each question or incomplete statement is followed by several suggested answers or completions. Select the one that BEST answers the question or completes the statement. *PRINT THE LETTER OF THE CORRECT ANSWER IN THE SPACE AT THE RIGHT.*

1. In the economy of the United States, the actual gross national product is most likely to be less than the potential GNP at full capacity whenever

    A. business investment is large
    B. consumer spending is rising
    C. government spending is falling
    D. total spending is falling

2. _____ would tend to reduce consumer spending.

    A. A reduction in personal income tax rates
    B. A decline in consumer incomes
    C. An expectation that prices will soon rise
    D. Increased government payments to individuals

3. When the economy fluctuates between boom and depression, the part of *total* spending that changes by the largest percent is

    A. spending by families on consumer goods and services
    B. business spending on factories, machinery, and inventories
    C. state and local government spending on all activities
    D. business spending on wages and salaries

4. If, when there is full employment, the federal government increases its spending WITHOUT increasing its tax revenues, *generally*

    A. a serious depression will occur
    B. an increase in unemployment will occur
    C. the national debt will decrease
    D. inflation will occur

5. A government budgetary deficit exists whenever

    A. the national debt is decreasing
    B. taxes are reduced
    C. government expenditures are increased
    D. total government spending exceeds receipts

6. When more money is created through government mints or through increased bank lending, the result is *generally*

    A. more spending   B. less spending
    C. higher interest rates   D. decreased savings

7. The Federal Reserve Board *generally* tries to increase the money supply when it wants to

    A. fight unemployment during recessions
    B. fight inflation
    C. hold down the government debt
    D. make large profits

8. The limit of an economy's real output at any time is set by

    A. business demand for goods and services
    B. the quantity and quality of labor, capital, and natural resources
    C. government regulations and spending
    D. the amount of money in circulation

9. MOST of the funds on deposit in commercial banks originate through

    A. individuals depositing currency in banks
    B. the rise of our gold stock
    C. business firms extending credit to customers
    D. banks making loans and investments

10. A monetary policy is *often* ineffective when used to check a recession, because at such times

    A. banks lack reserves to make loans
    B. there may NOT be a strong demand for loans
    C. the Federal Reserve CANNOT engage in open-market conditions
    D. reserve requirements CANNOT be lowered

11. Rapidly growing economies differ from slowly growing economies in that the former are always characterized by a(n)

    A. slow rate of population growth
    B. abundant supply of natural resources
    C. high rate of investment
    D. balanced national budget

12. If effective demand (i.e., total spending) periodically falls short of productive capacity, the rate of growth of the economy over a long period will be _____ because

    A. higher; inefficient plants, equipment, and labor no longer need be employed
    B. higher; production will be concentrated on necessary goods rather than luxuries
    C. lower; some productive resources will not be employed
    D. lower; of a heavier reliance on the raw materials of foreign countries

13. Three of these statements are TRUE of the so-called underdeveloped economies. Which one is NOT?

    A. Approximately two-thirds of the world's population live in such areas.
    B. These areas would soon achieve developed economies if their domestic money supply could be greatly increased.
    C. Low income in these areas makes savings for economic growth difficult.
    D. Political and social conditions exist that hold back their economic development.

14. *Americans are a mixed-up people with no sense of ethical values. Everyone knows that baseball is far less necessary than food and steel, yet they pay ballplayers a lot more than farmers and steelworkers.*
    Why?   14._____

    A. Ballplayers are *really* entertainers rather than producers.
    B. Ballplayers are more skilled than persons who get less pay.
    C. Excellent baseball players are scarcer relative to the demand for their services.
    D. There are fewer professional ballplayers than farmers or steelworkers.

15. The median household income in the United States in 2013 was between _____ and _____.   15._____

    A. $20,000; $30,000   B. $30,000; $40,000
    C. $40,000; $60,000   D. $60,000; $80,000

16. In the United States, the high wages received by MOST workers depend *largely* on   16._____

    A. actions of the federal government
    B. the social responsibility shown by business
    C. our minimum wage laws
    D. the high output per worker

17. Labor unions in the United States have   17._____

    A. strengthened the bargaining position of laborers in relation to their employers
    B. substantially increased the real wages of organized labor as compared with those of unorganized labor
    C. increased the percent of Americans who earn their living by rendering labor services
    D. increased competition in the labor market

18. The government program for agriculture is BEST summarized in which statement?   18._____

    A. Output has been drastically reduced so that surpluses have not accumulated; thus, farm income and prices of farm products have been high.
    B. An attempt has been made to improve farm incomes by taking a variety of measures to raise the price of farm products above the free market price.
    C. The government pays farmers enough money to bring their yearly incomes after taxes up to the level of incomes received by average non-farm laborers.
    D. Ours has been a policy of laissez-faire – of expressing concern for the farmer but generally doing nothing to affect the level of his income.

19. Identify the FALSE explanation of the *farm problem* in the United States.   19._____

    A. The growth of agricultural productivity has been much less rapid than that of the rest of the economy.
    B. Technological change has made it economical to use less labor and more capital in agriculture.
    C. As our economy has grown, the total demand for agricultural products has increased much less than for industrial products.
    D. When farm prices fall, the consumption of agricultural products increases only slightly.

20. Of these features of capitalism, communism as practiced in the former Soviet Union functioned without

    A. prices
    B. capital goods
    C. private profit
    D. all of the above

21. Which point is characteristic of both communism as practiced in the U.S.S.R. and private enterprise as practiced in the United States?

    A. Nearly all capital goods and natural resources are owned by the state.
    B. Trade unions have an important role in setting wages and conditions of work.
    C. Market prices automatically reflect consumer demand.
    D. Differences in money wages and salaries are used as an economic incentive.

22. As compared with more orthodox, communism, democratic socialism (e.g., in the United Kingdom, Sweden, and India)

    A. has more extensive government control over wages
    B. uses wage incentives more for workers
    C. places more emphasis on rapid economic growth
    D. permits the people more influence over what is produced

Questions 23-25.

DIRECTIONS: Questions 23 to 25 refer to the three charts on the next page.

23. Judging from your inspection of the charts above, the MOST serious economic problem of the early 1960's seems to be the

    A. decline in the output of the economy
    B. rapid inflation
    C. unemployment
    D. increase of the gross national product to a new all-time high

24. The fact that the consumer price index on the chart was *approximately* 75 in 1947 means that the average price of consumer goods and services in 1947 was about

    A. 75¢ a unit
    B. 75% above the average level of prices since 1947
    C. 25% less than 1957-59 prices
    D. 75% lower than at present

25. On the charts above, note the behavior of the economy between 1956 and 1958. Which statement MOST correctly analyzes the situation and states the MOST appropriate monetary and fiscal policies for these years?

    A. With GNP moving to an all-time high, *no* change in policy is necessary to keep the economy stable.
    B. Unemployment is rising. A budgetary deficit and/or an easy money policy is called for.
    C. Inflation continues and accelerates. A budgetary surplus and/or a tight money policy is called for.
    D. A dilemma exists. The appropriate monetary-fiscal policy to reduce unemployment is *likely* to increase the inflation, and policies to check inflation may increase unemployment.

GROSS NATIONAL PRODUCT, PRICES AND UNEMPLOYMENT

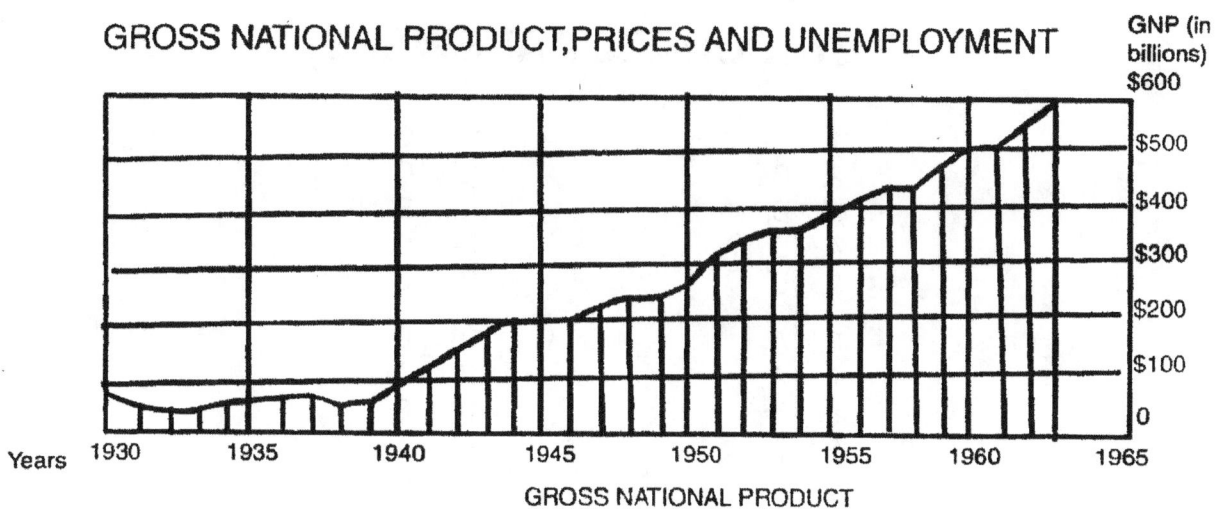
GROSS NATIONAL PRODUCT

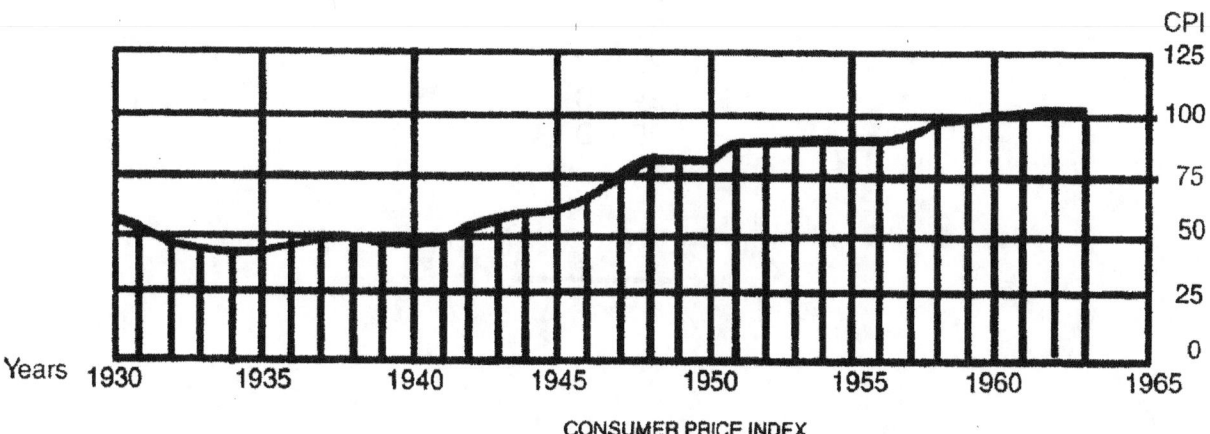
CONSUMER PRICE INDEX
(1957-59=100)

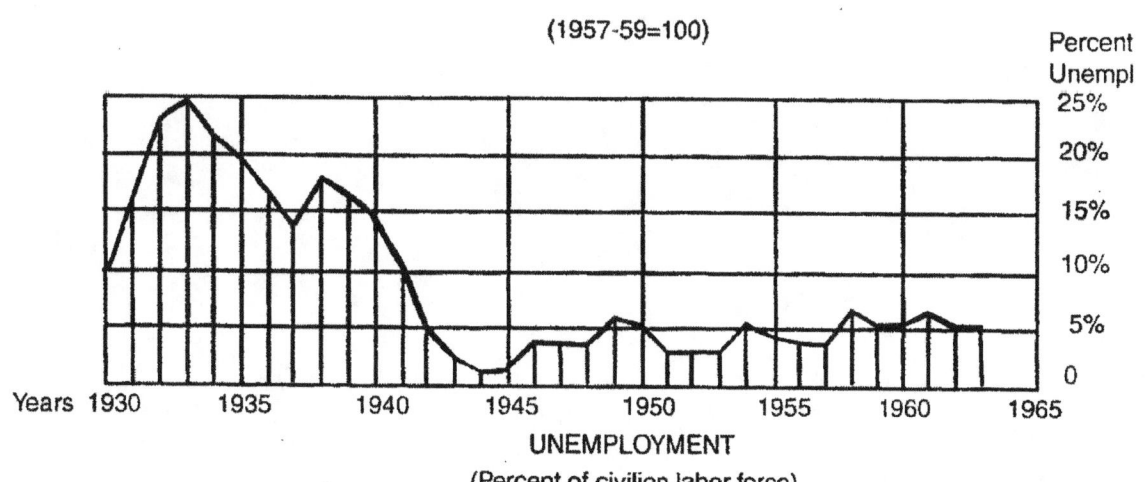
UNEMPLOYMENT
(Percent of civilion labor force)

KEY (CORRECT ANSWERS)

1.	D	11.	C
2.	B	12.	C
3.	B	13.	B
4.	D	14.	C
5.	D	15.	C
6.	A	16.	D
7.	A	17.	A
8.	B	18.	B
9.	D	19.	A
10.	B	20.	C

21. D
22. D
23. C
24. C
25. D

TEST 2

DIRECTIONS: Each question or incomplete statement is followed by several suggested answers or completions. Select the one that BEST answers the question or completes the statement. *PRINT THE LETTER OF THE CORRECT ANSWER IN THE SPACE AT THE RIGHT.*

1. When a nation's human and material resources are being fully and efficiently used, more of any one product

   A. cannot be produced
   B. cannot be produced unless private enterprise rather than government does so
   C. can be produced only if there is less production of some other products
   D. can be produced only if there is a general decrease in prices

   1.____

2. All economic systems (capitalist, communist, feudal, or any other) face similar economic problems.
   Which one of these questions would SOME but not all economies face?

   A. What will be produced and how?
   B. How can markets be kept competitive?
   C. How many resources will be devoted to maintaining and increasing future capacity?
   D. For whom will the goods be produced?

   2.____

3. In a basically private enterprise economy, which group exercises the PRINCIPAL influence on the choice of goods produced over a long period of time?

   A. Consumers   B. Government
   C. Big business   D. Labor unions

   3.____

4. Which is NOT a function of profits in a basically private enterprise economy?

   A. Providing an incentive for efficient production by businesses
   B. Rewarding producers who give consumers what they demand
   C. Inducing businessmen to assume necessary business risks
   D. Indicating to the government where wages are too low

   4.____

5. How does a family's saving MOST clearly influence capital formation?

   A. Saving means spending less; therefore, family saving hurts the seller and thus discourages capital formation.
   B. Savings are ALWAYS invested by the saver; therefore, an increase in family saving increases capital formation.
   C. A family's savings are normally channeled through financial institutions to firms that *usually* use the savings for capital formation.
   D. A family's savings lead to capital formation when they are used to pay off debts.

   5.____

6. In a basically private enterprise economy, the MAIN objective of businessmen is to

   A. provide good jobs for workers at reasonable wages
   B. secure government regulation that is favorable to business
   C. try to make profits
   D. provide highest-quality products

   6.____

7. If a consumer is to exercise his freedom of choice wisely in a private enterprise economy, he

   A. should know whether a product was produced by a monopolist
   B. MUST know where products are produced so that he may purchase those made locally, if possible
   C. should know what alternative goods and services are available as well as their qualities and prices
   D. MUST have sufficient income to permit him to purchase whatever he chooses

7.____

8. Assume that the demand increases for a commodity produced by many competitive firms.
   The resulting rise in price of the commodity will *usually* lead to

   A. less being produced
   B. more being produced
   C. no change in production
   D. elimination of inefficient businesses from the market

8.____

9. If the supply of a commodity increases at the same time the demand for it falls, in the absence of counteracting forces, its price will

   A. rise
   B. fall
   C. stay the same
   D. be indeterminate

9.____

10. In a private enterprise economy, the public interest is served even when individuals pursue their own private economic goals.
    This is because of

    A. the social responsibility of private businessmen
    B. careful planning and coordination of economic activity
    C. the operation of competitive markets
    D. individuals who understand what is in the public interest

10.____

11. Under a private enterprise economy, the function of competition is to

    A. eliminate wasteful advertising
    B. eliminate interest and profits
    C. prevent large firms from driving small ones out of business
    D. force prices to the LOWEST level consistent with a reasonable profit

11.____

12. Of these factors, a(n) _____ is *not likely* to increase the demand for bricks.

    A. increase in the price of home construction
    B. increase in the incomes of potential home builders
    C. decrease in the price of mortar (i.e., a complementary commodity)
    D. increase in the price of lumber (i.e., a substitute for bricks)

12.____

13. Which of the following is the MOST basic economic objection to monopolies?

    A. Prices set by monopolies are *usually* too low.
    B. Monopolies exert disproportionate political power.
    C. When a monopoly fails, the effect upon our economy is far more serious than when a competitive enterprise fails.
    D. Economic resources will tend to be less efficiently allocated.

13.____

14. Identify the FALSE statement regarding the economy of the United States over the past fifty years.

    A. Monopoly has increased to the point where it controls more than half of our production.
    B. The average size of firms has grown substantially.
    C. Small firms and large firms have both increased in number.
    D. Improved transportation and communication have resulted in firms competing over larger markets.

15. The federal government attempts to eliminate monopolies MAINLY in order to

    A. ensure competition
    B. prevent small firms from decreasing
    C. expand public utilities
    D. prevent the growth of big business

16. In large business corporations, the common stockholders *generally* do NOT

    A. own the business
    B. receive a share of the profits
    C. vote for the board of directors
    D. manage the day-to-day business

17. The opportunity cost (or alternative cost) of a new public high school is the

    A. money cost of the new building
    B. other desirable economic goods that must be forgone to secure the school
    C. necessary increase in the annual tax rate
    D. cost of constructing it now as opposed to the cost of a new school at a later date

18. Government expenditures (federal, state, and local combined) *now* represent about what portion of the gross national product?

    A. A tenth
    B. A quarter
    C. Half
    D. Three-fourths

19. The bulk of federal government expenditure during the Reagan-Bush years was for

    A. foreign aid
    B. the space program
    C. special benefits for the poor and unemployed
    D. national defense

20. In a basically private enterprise economy, a(n) _____ is *likely* to alter MOST the pattern of consumer choice among alternative products.

    A. general sales tax
    B. personal income tax
    C. excise tax on particular products
    D. tax on business profits

21. Specialization and exchange within a nation or between nations create which effect?

    A. A larger total quantity of wanted goods and services can be produced.
    B. The independence of both nations and individuals is increased.
    C. The danger of economic instability is reduced.
    D. All costs of production will rise, but not proportionately.

22. When a nation is running a deficit in its international balance of payments, it is ALWAYS currently

    A. exporting more goods than it is importing
    B. importing more goods than it is exporting
    C. paying more to other nations than others are paying to it
    D. helping less fortunate nations to develop economically

23. Reduced U.S. tariffs would *probably*

    A. lessen job opportunities in our export industries
    B. injure most farmers
    C. force some workers out of jobs in presently protected industries
    D. lower the average U.S. standard of living

24. When obtained at various intervals, which one of these four types of statistics will give the BEST measure of the economic growth of a nation?

    A. Balance of payments   B. Index of stock prices
    C. Total employment   D. Real income per capita

25. Annual gross national product is a measure of

    A. the quantity of goods and services produced by private businesses
    B. the value of a nation's total output of goods and services
    C. the price level of goods and services sold
    D. that part of production which is used by the government

KEY (CORRECT ANSWERS)

1. C
2. B
3. A
4. D
5. C

6. C
7. C
8. B
9. B
10. C

11. D
12. A
13. D
14. A
15. A

16. D
17. B
18. B
19. D
20. C

21. A
22. C
23. C
24. D
25. B

TEST 3

DIRECTIONS: Each question or incomplete statement is followed by several suggested answers or completions. Select the one that BEST answers the question or completes the statement. *PRINT THE LETTER OF THE CORRECT ANSWER IN THE SPACE AT THE RIGHT.*

1. The MAXIMUM gross national product a nation can produce in any one year is set by

   A. its natural resources
   B. families' demand for products
   C. the amount of money people have to spend
   D. its productive resources

2. Often an economy operates at less than full employment. This is *most likely* to occur when

   A. total spending is inadequate
   B. there is inflation
   C. there is a scarcity of unskilled labor
   D. ever competition is intense.

3. The *total* output of the economy is bought by which large group of spenders?

   A. Farmers, laborers, and housewives
   B. Consumers, business firms, and governments
   C. Investors, speculators, and bankers
   D. Corporations, households, and capitalists

4. In recessions in the United States since World War II, _____ has declined MOST sharply.

   A. family spending on consumer goods
   B. business firms' spending on plants, equipment, and inventories
   C. family spending on services
   D. government spending on goods and services

5. Increasing the government budgetary surplus or decreasing the deficit is particularly desirable in a period of

   A. inflation
   B. mass unemployment
   C. depression
   D. economic instability

6. The PRIMARY reason for the growth in federal debt over the last century has been government deficits caused by

   A. wasteful domestic expenditures and social welfare payments
   B. depressions and recessions
   C. declining tax receipts
   D. wars

7. An increase in the amount of money in the nation *usually* leads to higher prices EXCEPT when

   A. there is widespread unemployment of men and machines
   B. labor unions are strong
   C. the nation's gold reserves are adequate
   D. there is general prosperity

8. When commercial banks increase their loans to businesses and consumers, the result is a(n)

   A. decrease in the spending power of consumers and businesses
   B. increase in the nation's money supply
   C. increase in government control over the economy
   D. increase in the banks' excess reserves

9. In an inflationary period, an appropriate policy for the Federal Reserve would be to

   A. sell government securities on the open market
   B. lower legal reserve requirements
   C. decrease the discount rate
   D. encourage member banks to increase their loans

10. _____ are typically hurt the MOST by inflation.

    A. Farmers
    B. Debtors
    C. Government bondholders
    D. Businessmen

11. Assume our economy is operating at full capacity.
    Which policy would NOT be appropriate to increase our rate of economic growth?

    A. Encouraging an increase of private savings and investment in capital goods and equipment
    B. Improving the skill and knowledge of people through increased education
    C. Developing technology and managerial ability
    D. Encouraging an increase in personal consumption

12. If total demand declines relative to the productive capacity of the economy,

    A. the growth rate is *likely* to slow down, at least temporarily
    B. inflation is *likely* to occur
    C. a large government budgetary surplus is *likely* to occur
    D. employment is *likely* to increase

13. The average per capita income of the two-thirds of the world's population in the so-called underdeveloped nations is _____ of ours.

    A. less than one-tenth
    B. about one-quarter
    C. about one-half
    D. about three-fourths

14. The MOST general cause of low individual incomes in the United States is

    A. lack of valuable productive services to sell
    B. unwillingness to work
    C. automation
    D. discrimination against non-union employees

15. In the United States during the present decade,

    A. inequality in personal incomes has been *largely* eliminated
    B. the rich have become richer and the poor poorer
    C. average real family income after taxes has remained *generally* unchanged
    D. income inequality has been *somewhat* reduced

16. High wages in the United States are based on the high productivity of U.S. labor. All of these factors contribute to this high productivity EXCEPT

    A. the skill and work habits of U.S. labor
    B. our accumulation of a large stock of capital goods
    C. our technological and managerial advances
    D. tariff protection from competition of low-paid foreign workers

17. Both featherbedding by unions and monopolistic practices by employers are *likely* to result in

    A. an increase in average labor productivity for the nation as a whole
    B. a less efficient use of resources
    C. less labor being used in the industry affected
    D. a raising of average real wages in the nation as a whole

18. Identify the MOST obvious result of our governmental policy toward agriculture.

    A. The average farm income has been raised *almost* to the level of the average non-farm income.
    B. Large surpluses of farm commodities have been accumulated by the government.
    C. Capital and labor have turned to agriculture to take advantage of guaranteed high prices and profits.
    D. The family farm has been *almost* completely replaced by the large corporate farm.

19. Measures to increase economic security against unemployment will tend to increase economic efficiency if

    A. one cannot transfer to better-paying jobs offered by other employers, to be eligible for benefits
    B. the security the measure provides tends to reduce one's incentive to produce
    C. the costs of the measures are borne equally by firms regardless of their record for causing economic insecurity
    D. the average output per worker is increased as a result of improved economic security

20. In the United States, in contrast to socialist/communist nations,

    A. the problem of scarcity has been eliminated
    B. consumer spending *largely* determines what commodities are produced
    C. incomes are unequally distributed
    D. government plays an insignificant role in economic life

4 (#3)

21. The interest rate charged on overnight loans from one member bank of the Federal Reserve System to another is known as

    A. overnight fund interest rate
    B. exdividend rate
    C. Federal funds rate
    D. fiscal debenture reserve rate

22. Compared with the U.S. economy, the democratic socialist economies of the United Kingdom, the Scandinavian countries, and India

    A. are considerably more productive
    B. have more government ownership and control
    C. demonstrate clearly that *only* private enterprise is compatible with democracy
    D. have been short-lived, for in two of the cases socialism has been abandoned

Questions 23-25.

DIRECTIONS: Questions 23-25 refer to the charts on the on the following page.

23. We desire a growing economy in which the price level is stable and employment reasonably high.
    The charts on the preceding page show that we have MOST fully approximated this ideal between _____ and _____.

    A. 1937; 1938
    B. 1940; 1941
    C. 1946; 1947
    D. 1955; 1956

24. Judging from your inspection of the three charts, the MOST serious economic problem of the immediate postwar period (1946-48) is

    A. decline in the output of the economy
    B. inflation
    C. unemployment
    D. declining output per worker

25. On the charts, note the behavior of the economy between 1950 and 1952.
    Identify the statement which MOST correctly analyzes the situation and states the MOST appropriate monetary and fiscal policies for these years.

    A. The GNP is moving to an all-time high and prices are stable; no change in policy is called for.
    B. Unemployment is rising; a budgetary deficit and/or an easy money policy is called for.
    C. It is a period of inflation; a budgetary surplus and/or a tight money policy is called for.
    D. Employment is falling and prices are rising; therefore, a budgetary deficit and/or a tight money policy is called for.

5 (#3)

GROSS NATIONAL PRODUCT, PRICES AND UNEMPLOYMENT

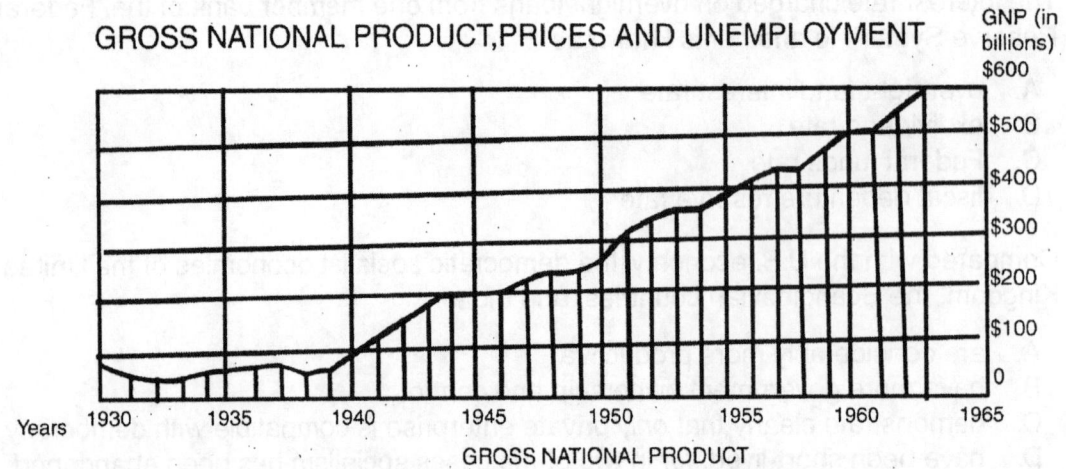

GROSS NATIONAL PRODUCT

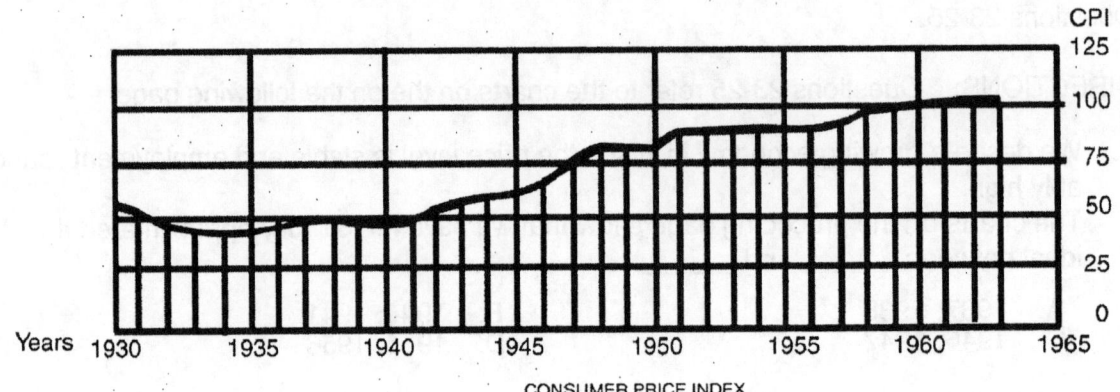

CONSUMER PRICE INDEX
(1957-59=100)

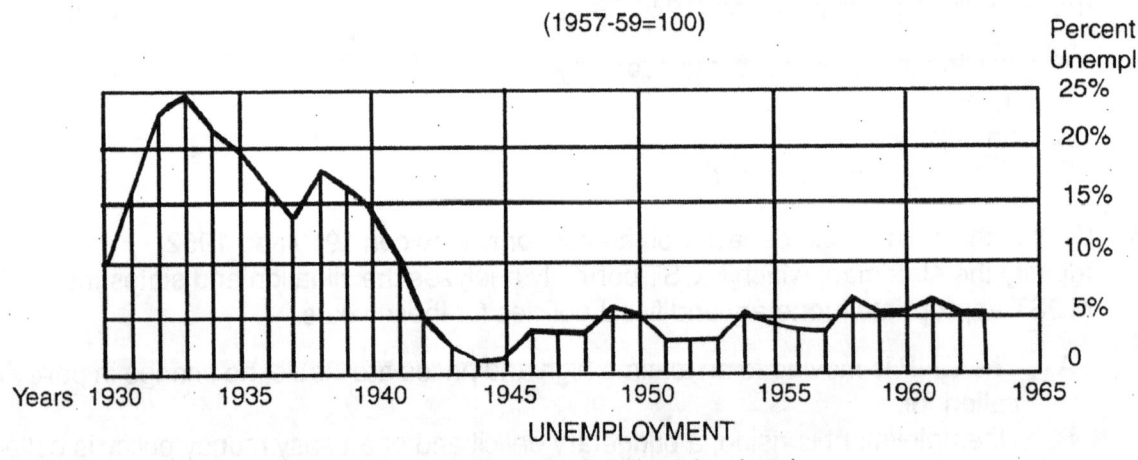

UNEMPLOYMENT
(Percent of civilion labor force)

KEY (CORRECT ANSWERS)

1. D
2. A
3. B
4. B
5. A

6. D
7. A
8. B
9. A
10. C

11. D
12. A
13. A
14. A
15. D

16. D
17. B
18. B
19. D
20. B

21. C
22. B
23. D
24. B
25. C

TEST 4

DIRECTIONS: Each question or incomplete statement is followed by several suggested answers or completions. Select the one that BEST answers the question or completes the statement. *PRINT THE LETTER OF THE CORRECT ANSWER IN THE SPACE AT THE RIGHT.*

1. Every economic system faces the need to economize. In this context, the BEST definition of *to economize* is to

   A. save money and thus reduce the national debt
   B. dispense with the production of luxuries
   C. balance the government's budget by reducing spending
   D. make the best use of scarce resources that have alternative uses

2. What is meant by the assertion that *every* economic system (such as socialism, capitalism, communism) faces the fact of scarcity?

   A. There are insufficient productive resources to satisfy all wants of a society.
   B. There are times when some products can be had *only* by paying high prices.
   C. In the beginning, every society faces shortages, but a mature economy, such as our own, overcomes scarcity in time.
   D. All economies have depressions during which scarcities exist.

3. Which point BEST characterizes the relation between producers, consumers, and government in a private enterprise economy?

   A. Producers decide what to produce, government how it shall be produced, and consumers who shall receive the product.
   B. Consumer spending leads producers to decide what shall be produced and how resources shall be used. Government seeks to maintain competition and the rights of private property.
   C. Consumers decide what should be produced, producers how BEST to produce it, and government who shall receive which products.
   D. Government ultimately decides what shall be produced and how. Consumers and producers, as voters, control the government.

4. Three of the following are essential to the operation of a private enterprise economy. Which one might such an economy operate WITHOUT?

   A. Profit motive   B. Markets
   C. Corporations   D. Prices

5. The principle of diminishing returns is BEST illustrated by

   A. small firms being driven out of business by large firms
   B. any decline in the average rate of profits
   C. a slowing rate of increase in output as a farmer adds increasing amounts of fertilizer to his land
   D. the decline in personal income as workers age

6. Business firms wish to sell their products at a high price; households wish to buy products at low prices.
   In a private enterprise economy, this conflict of interests

   A. is reconciled by competitive markets
   B. is reconciled by government regulation
   C. does NOT exist; there is really *no* conflict of interest between households and firms
   D. is NOT reconciled; since all household heads are members of firms, the interests of firms prevail

7. In a private enterprise economy, government encourages freedom of choice by

   A. guaranteeing complete freedom of choice to households and firms
   B. limiting this freedom for some if their choices might reduce freedom of choice significantly for others
   C. requiring individuals and firms to use their freedom of choice wisely
   D. seeing that individuals and firms choose what the majority believes BEST

8. A rise in the price of _____ would be *likely* to increase the demand for butter.

   A. butter
   B. oleomargarine
   C. bread
   D. any of the above

9. Assuming that the supply of a product remains constant as the demand for it increases, its price will *normally*

   A. fall
   B. rise
   C. stay the same
   D. either rise or fall

10. _____ is MOST essential for a private enterprise economy.

    A. Active competition in the marketplace
    B. The functioning of labor unions
    C. Action by responsible business leaders
    D. Extensive government regulation

11. The price of shoes is *likely* to be increased by

    A. more capital investment by producers
    B. a decrease in the demand for shoes
    C. a decrease in the supply of shoes
    D. new machines reducing the cost of shoe production

12. If the government were to levy a tax of one dollar on every pair of shoes sold, a *most likely* result would be that

    A. consumers would pay a higher price for shoes and probably buy a smaller quantity
    B. suppliers would increase the quantity sold in order to offset the taxes paid to the government
    C. consumers would pay a higher price and, as a result, suppliers would make larger profits
    D. suppliers would sell more and charge a higher price

13. Generally, when a monopoly replaces private competitive enterprises,

    A. production efficiency is increased because of the larger scale of operation
    B. the market *no* longer tends to bring about the MOST efficient allocation of resources
    C. there is an increase in the number of firms making the product
    D. the monopolist controls both consumers and labor

14. The purpose of the Sherman and Clayton Antitrust Acts is to

    A. keep markets effectively competitive
    B. keep firms from becoming large
    C. prevent banks from becoming trusts
    D. protect the investing public

15. Common stocks, limited liability, and a charter are characteristic of

    A. individual proprietorships
    B. partnerships
    C. private business corporations
    D. most small business firms

16. Over the past fifty years, the share of the total U.S. market controlled by the hundred largest firms has

    A. changed by only a small amount
    B. risen substantially
    C. increased to more than 90 percent
    D. fallen steadily

17. These arguments have been used regarding the proposals for increased public expenditures on education.
    Which one shows the BEST use of economic reasoning, using the alternative (or opportunity cost) principle?

    A. Taxpayers should compare the probable sacrifices resulting from the added tax with the probable advantages of the new program.
    B. In real terms, the added school tax will cost us necessary food and clothing, adequate support of our churches, and essential medical care.
    C. Luxuries are the real alternative cost of the proposed educational improvements.
    D. Whenever a product is good, public or private expenditure on it is always desirable.

18. Government expenditure (federal, state, and local combined) is now the GREATEST for

    A. social services, including health and social security
    B. salaries of elected public officials, upkeep of public buildings, and cost of hearings, of the court system, and of highways
    C. public education - elementary, secondary, and higher
    D. national defense and related operations

19. Most taxes divert spending power; as a result, control over some resources passes from

    A. the government to individuals and businesses
    B. individuals and businesses to government

C. the federal government to the state government
D. gross national product to national income

20. Given our present pattern of government expenditure, the graduated or progressive income tax causes 20.____

    A. income after taxes to be more evenly distributed
    B. the rich to get richer and the poor to get poorer
    C. wage earners to pay more tax than property owners
    D. it to be impossible to inherit wealth

21. Specialization and division of labor by nations followed by increasing international trade *probably* would 21.____

    A. increase total world production of wanted goods and services
    B. lower living standards in the wealthy nations
    C. increase the likelihood of worldwide unemployment
    D. eliminate differences in standards of living among nations

22. A nation has a deficit in its international balance of payments when it 22.____

    A. buys more goods and services abroad than it sells
    B. makes more payments, excluding gold, to other countries than it receives from them
    C. has an unfavorable balance of trade
    D. owes more gold to other nations than it has

23. Each statement about tariffs is *likely* to be TRUE EXCEPT that tariffs 23.____

    A. preserve employment in domestic industries whose products they protect
    B. reduce the market for our exports by reducing our imports
    C. encourage the growth of our most efficient industries and eliminate the least efficient
    D. benefit some groups at the expense of the national standard of living

24. Inflation is *most likely* to benefit 24.____

    A. savings bank depositors
    B. debtors
    C. life insurance policyholders
    D. persons living on fixed pensions

25. The BEST single measure of the total economic output in the United States is the 25.____

    A. gross national product
    B. total amount of take-home pay
    C. consumer price index
    D. index of industrial production

KEY (CORRECT ANSWERS)

1.	D	11.	C
2.	A	12.	A
3.	B	13.	B
4.	C	14.	A
5.	C	15.	C
6.	A	16.	A
7.	B	17.	A
8.	B	18.	D
9.	B	19.	B
10.	A	20.	A

21. A
22. B
23. C
24. B
25. A

EXAMINATION SECTION
TEST 1

DIRECTIONS: Each question or incomplete statement is followed by several suggested answers or completions. Select the one that BEST answers the question or completes the statement. *PRINT THE LETTER OF THE CORRECT ANSWER IN THE SPACE AT THE RIGHT.*

1. The MAIN advantage associated with a producer's use of a wholesaler's services is 1.____

    A. control of product promotion
    B. product security
    C. freedom to concentrate on production and development
    D. provision of an outside sales force

2. During the sales analysis process, a company's sales are broken down into fundamental units of 2.____

    A. dollar volume   B. transactions
    C. revenue   D. market share

3. A retailer wants to use a wholesaler that will perform purchasing and stocking functions for the outlet, and who will take back unsold products. What type of wholesaler should the retailer use? 3.____

    A. Rack jobber   B. Drop shipper
    C. Mail order   D. Truck

4. Which of the following is an example of convenience goods? 4.____

    A. Major appliance   B. Automobile
    C. Detergent   D. Clothing

5. A company decides to conduct an audit of its marketing productivity. Which of the following questions is it likely to ask? 5.____

    A. How logical are the company's objectives, given the more significant opportunities or threats and its relative resources?
    B. Can the organization handle the planning needed at the individual product/brand level?
    C. How well does the product line meet the line's objective?
    D. How profitable are each of the company's products or brands?

6. From the microeconomic point of view, the basic regulator of any free-market economic system is 6.____

    A. supply   B. demand   C. income   D. price

7. Which of the following is a type of sales promotion that is used *primarily* with newly introduced products? 7.____

    A. Premiums   B. Consumer sweepstakes
    C. Free samples   D. Sales contests

121

8. Compared to other characteristics involved in predicting consumer buying behavior, demographics are less

   A. reliable
   B. actionable
   C. subjective
   D. available

9. Which of the following practices is NOT specifically prohibited by the Clayton Act?

   A. Price discrimination
   B. Contracts in restraint of trade
   C. Interlocking directorates
   D. Intercorporate stockholdings

10. A retail product assortment is generally evaluated in terns of each of the following EXCEPT

    A. status
    B. margin
    C. completeness
    D. purpose

11. In general, which of the following is NOT one of the essential elements of an enforceable contract, whether written or unwritten?

    A. Consideration
    B. Transfer of goods or services
    C. Subject matter
    D. Capacity of parties

12. The most traditional marketing channel for consumer products is producer

    A. consumer →
    B. retailer → consumer
    C. wholesaler → retailer → consumer
    D. agent or broker → wholesaler → retailer → consumer

13. The primary *disadvantage* associated with personal selling is that

    A. smaller companies will not be able to justify many sales expenditures
    B. it generally costs more than media advertising for smaller companies
    C. the sales representative can communicate with only a relatively small number of potential customers
    D. smaller companies cannot manage geographic coverage of a region

14. Which of the following products, purchased by an individual consumer, is MOST likely to be selected through routine response behavior?

    A. Laundry detergent
    B. Clothing
    C. Kitchen appliance
    D. Electric drill

15. Typically, physical distribution costs will account for approximately _____% of a product's retail price.

    A. 5
    B. 10
    C. 20
    D. 30

16. A _____ generally operates within the smallest geographical limits.

    A. broker
    B. selling agent
    C. manufacturer's agent
    D. commission merchant

17. Which of the following is NOT a significant reason why companies continually introduce new product lines sometimes in spite of their own highly successful products?

    A. Anticipation of unpredictable environmental or competitive changes
    B. High failure rates for most new products
    C. Company emphasis on investment capital
    D. A concern for long-term growth

18. Compared to industrial demand, consumer demand is NOT

    A. elastic
    B. joint
    C. derived
    D. more fluctuating

19. The MOST common method of evaluating sales performance is

    A. marketing audit
    B. marketing cost analysis
    C. functional analysis
    D. sales analysis

20. An intermediary serves a marketing channel by breaking down homogeneous stocks into smaller units for wholesalers and retailers. Which sorting activity is being performed by the intermediary?

    A. Sorting out
    B. Accumulation
    C. Allocation
    D. Assorting

21. The strategy of intensive distribution would MOST likely be used in the marketing of

    A. shopping goods
    B. perishable goods
    C. specialized services
    D. convenience goods

22. A company's potential customers are large in size, but few in number, and the company's promotional resources are limited. The company's personal selling objective would MOST likely be to

    A. develop new customers
    B. provide technical service to facilitate sales
    C. maintain customer loyalty
    D. win acceptance for new products

23. A consumer sees an advertisement in a magazine and ignores the photograph and caption. Instead the customer directs her attention directly to the printed matter below the image.
    This is an example of

    A. selective retention
    B. misperception
    C. selective distortion
    D. selective exposure

24. For a strategic business unit, the adoption of a marketing management structure is MOST appropriate when

    A. the product management structure is not used as a training ground for top management
    B. a single product may be market to a large number of different markets where customers have very different requirements and preferences
    C. a business faces an extremely complex and uncertain environment
    D. products and markets are few and similar in nature

25. The Uniform Commercial Code (UCC) is NOT intended to

    A. shift the emphasis away from the concept of property to the concept of contract
    B. make laws uniform among various jurisdictions
    C. establish recommendations for handling warranty or product liability disputes
    D. simplify and de-emphasize the concept of title determination

KEY (CORRECT ANSWERS)

1.	C	11.	B
2.	B	12.	C
3.	A	13.	C
4.	C	14.	A
5.	D	15.	C
6.	D	16.	C
7.	C	17.	C
8.	C	18.	A
9.	B	19.	D
10.	B	20.	C

21. D
22. D
23. D
24. B
25. C

TEST 2

DIRECTIONS: Each question or incomplete statement is followed by several suggested answers or completions. Select the one that BEST answers the question or completes the statement. *PRINT THE LETTER OF THE CORRECT ANSWER IN THE SPACE AT THE RIGHT.*

1. Subject to federal trademark law, the use requirement for a service mark is generally satisfied by display 1.____

   A. on the premises where the services are actually rendered
   B. on products associated with, or used for the purpose of, rendering the registered services
   C. in the sale or advertising of the service (and the services so identified are actually rendered)
   D. on a printed receipt of payment for the services rendered

2. In an organizational buying center, the buying process is MOST often initiated by 2.____

   A. influencers   B. gatekeepers
   C. users   D. buyers

3. A company's sales of a product, stated as a percentage of an entire industry's sales of the product, is referred to as the company's 3.____

   A. channel spot   B. market share
   C. net percentage   D. sector

4. The concept of product life cycle generally influences marketing management in each of the following ways EXCEPT 4.____

   A. a firm must generate new products or enter new markets to sustain its profitability over time
   B. objectives and strategy for a given product change as it passes through various life-cycle stages
   C. opportunities and threats in each stage aid in the formulation of a most appropriate marketing mix for each stage of the life cycle
   D. products in the maturity stage serve as a model for companies to maintain near-constant brand loyalty

5. When a company decides to market a new product, the last step before commercialization is typically 5.____

   A. test marketing   B. business analysis
   C. product development D. in-home testing

6. What is the term for the combination of two or more stages of a marketing channel under one management? 6.____

   A. Consolidation
   B. Vertical channel integration
   C. Allocation
   D. Horizontal channel integration

7. What is the most centralized and formalized organizational form within a strategic business unit of a company?

   A. Product management
   B. Matrix
   C. Market management
   D. Functional

8. A marketing department divides an industrial market according to the organizational characteristics of the customers. This is an example of

   A. market aggregation strategy
   B. sectoring
   C. macrosegmentation
   D. microsegmentation

9. A large producer of paper goods decides to initiate a *count and recount* sales promotion among its resellers. The promotion LEAST likely to be successful would be for those resellers

   A. who have small warehouses
   B. operating within a limited geographic area
   C. who deal in perishable goods
   D. with large and unwieldy distribution channels

10. On a market research questionnaire, a subject is asked to state the degree to which he agrees with the statement:
    Cable television is too expensive.
    What type of assessment is being made?

    A. Protective technique
    B. Depth interview
    C. Attitude scale
    D. Balloon test

11. For a strategic business unit of a company that has adopted a low-cost defender strategy, the business unit will

    A. perform best on volume and share growth when the structure has low levels of formalization and centralization
    B. experience high levels of inter-functional conflict
    C. perform best on volume and share growth when the structure has a high level of specialization
    D. perform best on cash flow when controller, financial, and production managers have a substantial influence on business and marketing strategy decisions

12. In selecting a new trademark, a company's choice will be aided materially by

    A. using the trademark as a root to form other words for example, by adding the suffixes *-ize* or *-ate*
    B. making sure the trademark's correct grammatical classification is as a proper adjective
    C. simply using the name of the product as part of all of the trademark
    D. using the trademark as a proper noun whenever possible

13. A warehouse showroom is a retail facility characterized by each of the following EXCEPT

    A. large on-premise inventory
    B. vertical merchandise display space

C. use of warehouse materials-handling technology
D. separate customer service departments

14. In market research, the psychographic study is used primarily to

    A. compartmentalize the respondents into different market segments
    B. occupy the respondent while his or her real preferences and behaviors are determined
    C. ask the respondent to describe the behavior or preferences of his or her own social group
    D. ask the respondent to describe his or her own behavior, preferences, and lifestyle

15. The strategy of exclusive distribution is suitable for each of the following types of products EXCEPT those that

    A. are consumed over a long period of time
    B. exist in a limited market
    C. are frequently purchased
    D. require service or information to fit them to buyers' needs

16. _____ goods are characterized by high price, limited distribution, and strong advertising.

    A. Specialty   B. Durable
    C. Shopping   D. Unsought

17. An example of capital goods is

    A. office furniture   B. fork lift
    C. electric motor   D. stationery

18. A company decides to alter its marketing strategy by protecting its position in the market and minimizing its investment. The company is in a _____ competitive position and the market is _____ attractive.

    A. strong; moderately   B. moderately; not very
    C. weak; not very   D. weak; highly

19. The extra cost a firm incurs when it produces one more unit of a product is termed _____ cost.

    A. marginal   B. average fixed
    C. unit   D. average variable

20. Which of the following is a condition that would NOT be conducive toward a business's adoption of a *market analyzer* strategy?

    A. New-product applications still possible
    B. Substantial competition
    C. Technological advances still possible
    D. Industry in introductory or growth stage of the product life cycle

21. Which of the following is NOT a marketer-dominated source of information to which a consumer might consult before making a purchase?

    A. Salespersons   B. Free samples
    C. Packaging   D. Displays

22. Generally, the practice of offering quantity discounts to a consumer is beneficial in each of the following ways EXCEPT.

    A. lower inventory costs for the seller
    B. lower costs of transportation and handling
    C. provides the opportunity for flexible pricing
    D. encouraging customers to place more business with a single seller

23. A large manufacturer wishes to establish a multi-stage marketing channel for its product, but encounters difficulty in securing the services of intermediary agents or wholesalers. The most likely reason is that

    A. the manufacturer is in a geographically unfavorable location
    B. distribution among middlemen is dominated by another channel leader
    C. the manufacturer's service reputation is poor
    D. consumer demand for the product is low

24. If an intermediary in a marketing channel performs the function of assorting, the intermediary is

    A. combining products into collections that buyers want
    B. developing a bank or stock of homogeneous products to provide aggregate inventory
    C. classifying heterogeneous supplies into homogeneous groups
    D. breaking down homogeneous stocks into smaller units for wholesalers and retailers

25. Which of the following types of wholesalers would be LEAST likely to provide a producer with information about market conditions?

    A. Truck
    B. Rack jobber
    C. Drop shipper
    D. Cash and carry

KEY (CORRECT ANSWERS)

1. C
2. C
3. B
4. D
5. A

6. B
7. D
8. C
9. A
10. C

11. D
12. B
13. D
14. D
15. C

16. A
17. B
18. B
19. A
20. D

21. B
22. C
23. B
24. A
25. D

TEST 3

DIRECTIONS: Each question or incomplete statement is followed by several suggested answers or completions. Select the one that BEST answers the question or completes the statement. *PRINT THE LETTER OF THE CORRECT ANSWER IN THE SPACE AT THE RIGHT.*

1. The profits for a company offering a certain product become *excessive,* meaning the company has the power to restrict its output in the short term. The most likely result of this would be   1.____

    A. the gradual disappearance from other competitors from the market, who cannot afford to similarly restrict output
    B. the erosion of the company's economic power due to increased supply from competitors
    C. a lengthening and widening of the product line
    D. a near-monopoly on the market for the product

2. An example of a direct cost is   2.____

    A. merchandising
    B. salesforce management
    C. general management
    D. cost of occupancy

3. Person-specific factors influencing consumer buying decisions are   3.____

    A. psychological and motivational
    B. demographic and situational
    C. psychological and social
    D. demographic and motivational

4. For a salesperson practicing technical selling, each of the following is generally considered to be an important personal characteristic EXCEPT   4.____

    A. education
    B. persuasiveness
    C. product knowledge
    D. customer knowledge

5. During physical distribution of a product, which of the following functions is LEAST likely to be computerized?   5.____

    A. Order entry
    B. Freight bill payment
    C. Invoicing
    D. Site location

6. For a marketing manager, the standard formula for improving cash flow management contains several elements. Which of the following is NOT one of these elements?   6.____

    A. Paying creditors quickly in order to eliminate interest costs
    B. Increasing the turnover of receivables by reducing the time taken by customers to pay their bills
    C. Reducing inventories
    D. Retaining a source of cash that requires no interest cost

7. The satisfaction of a trademark's *use in commerce,* subject to federal trademark law, is generally provided by the   7.____

    A. shipment of goods bearing the trademark across state or national boundaries
    B. application for trademark registration

C. affixation of the trademark to the products themselves, or to some portion of their containers or packaging
D. use of the registered trademark in advertising

8. Of all the methods used for analyzing marketing costs, the _____ cost approach is the least precise.

    A. full
    B. functional
    C. product-centered
    D. natural

9. Each of the following is an environmental factor that may influence an organization's buying behavior EXCEPT

    A. regulatory actions
    B. size and composition of buying center
    C. activities of interest groups
    D. inflation

10. For a business that adopts a prospecting strategy with respect to a certain market, which of the following policies would be most appropriate?

    A. Relatively narrow product lines
    B. Moderate to high trade promotion expenses as a percent of sales
    C. Relatively high degree of forward vertical integration
    D. Relatively low to competitive prices

11. Generally, the *mature* stage in a product's life cycle is characterized by

    A. large number of competitors
    B. high technical change in the product
    C. low profitability
    D. insignificant market growth rate

12. Dayton-Hudson, one of the country's largest retailers, has expanded from a regional department store into Target discount stores, B. Dalton bookstores, and several off-price fashion outlets.
    This is an example of

    A. horizontal channel integration
    B. accumulation
    C. vertical channel integration
    D. intensive distribution

13. A company might decide to engage in the practice of predatory pricing in order to

    A. segment a market in the early stages of a product life cycle
    B. generate a greater sales volume and lower production costs as much as possible
    C. enable a manufacturer to saturate a mass market quickly, before the competition can respond
    D. recover its high research-and-development costs more rapidly

14. A consumer displays the following patterns of buying behavior: He lives in a small house, favors national brands, spends more than other classes on household appliances, and is a heavy user of credit. According to market conventions, this consumer most likely occupies the _____ class.

    A. upper-middle
    B. lower-middle
    C. upper-lower
    D. lower-lower

15. Which of the following provisions was established by the Hart-Scott-Rodino Act of 1976?

    A. Prohibition of the acquisition of assets where the effect may be to create a monopoly
    B. Authorization of the FTC's issuance of trade regulation rules applicable to all members of an industry
    C. Authorization of FTC and Secretary of Health, Education and Welfare to issue regulations to ensure truthful disclosure of product identity and other relevant packaging practices
    D. Adoption of procedures to facilitate Department of Justice actions in antitrust actions

16. The MOST significant problem facing businesses who use the services of commission merchants is

    A. limited control over pricing
    B. short-term buyer-seller relationship
    C. limited geographic operations
    D. no delivery services

17. At different stages in a market's adoption of a new product, the role of personal influences is likely to be different. With this in mind, assume that the most influential source of information about a new farming product is U.S. Department of Agriculture field agent. The new product is most likely to be in the _____ stage of adoption.

    A. first awareness
    B. conception
    C. implementation
    D. decision

18. Typically, which of the following elements would appear LAST within an annual marketing plan?

    A. Key issues
    B. Projected profit-and-loss statement
    C. Controls
    D. Marketing strategy

19. According to the categories established by the VALS psychographic segments, the most disadvantaged Americans fall into the category of

    A. emulators
    B. sustainers
    C. belongers
    D. survivors

20. Over which of the following consumer buying selections would a reference group be LEAST likely to have influence?

    A. Cigarettes
    B. Insurance
    C. Canned peaches
    D. Headache remedy

21. One of the highest priorities for a producer in transporting its goods is security. If possible, which mode of transport should be selected?

    A. Air   B. Water   C. Rail   D. Truck

22. The simplest and often most effective way for a company to increase profitability while maintaining its current product mix is to

    A. find new customers
    B. extend the product line
    C. increase consumption among present consumers
    D. find new uses for the product

23. It is generally true that as the number of units produced by a company increases,

    A. production cost per unit decreases
    B. the company's capital investment in the product decreases
    C. the market will become more competitive
    D. demand will moderately increase

24. Which of the following is categorized as a psychological influence on the consumer buying decision process?

    A. Culture and subcultures
    B. Perception
    C. Demographic factors
    D. Roles and family influences

25. A company compensates its sales staff with a combination of straight salary and commission. For the company, the most significant *disadvantage* to this approach is

    A. necessity of closer supervision of salespersons' activities
    B. potential administration difficulties
    C. selling expenses remain constant during sales declines
    D. sales manager may lose control over sales force

KEY (CORRECT ANSWERS)

1. B
2. A
3. B
4. B
5. D

6. A
7. A
8. D
9. B
10. B

11. D
12. A
13. B
14. C
15. D

16. A
17. C
18. C
19. D
20. C

21. B
22. C
23. A
24. B
25. B

TEST 4

DIRECTIONS: Each question or incomplete statement is followed by several suggested answers or completions. Select the one that BEST answers the question or completes the statement. *PRINT THE LETTER OF THE CORRECT ANSWER IN THE SPACE AT THE RIGHT.*

1. One of the differences between marketing and selling is that marketing 1.____

    A. is a one-way process
    B. uses informal planning and feedback
    C. emphasizes groups of consumers
    D. is volume-oriented

2. It is NOT true that organizational consumers 2.____

    A. purchase on the basis of specifications and technical data
    B. rarely lease equipment
    C. are more likely than final consumers to apply value and vendor analysis
    D. have shorter distribution channels than final consumers

3. Which of the following is NOT an advantage of national brands? 3.____

    A. Less complicated to administer than private brands
    B. They are presold
    C. They stimulate promotion through rebates
    D. Selling materials are provided with the product

4. If changes in price are exactly offset by changes in quantity demanded, keeping sales revenue constant, _____ demand exists. 4.____

    A. derived   B. elastic   C. scaled   D. unitary

5. A dealer brand 5.____

    A. is usually only available in the outlets of a single retailer
    B. generally has the lowest relative price
    C. is focused on generating manufacturer control
    D. is usually of less overall quality as the manufacturer's brand

6. Which of the following is a disadvantage associated with simple trend analysis as a means of sales forecasting? 6.____

    A. Markets not representative of all locations
    B. Does not provide a means of forecasting
    C. Economic decline not considered
    D. It assumes a constant market share

7. Which of the following is NOT a typical source of information for a company's total variable costs? 7.____

    A. Estimates of labor productivity
    B. Cost data from suppliers
    C. Bills
    D. Sales estimates

8. A company decides to enter a new market with an older product. What type of strategy should be used by the marketing department?

   A. Market development
   B. Product development
   C. Diversification
   D. Market penetration

9. Which of the following is NOT an advantage associated with chain ownership of retail outlets?

   A. Strong management
   B. Low investment costs
   C. Larger market
   D. Central purchasing

10. Each of the following is a reason why modification of an existing product package might be necessitated EXCEPT

    A. curtailment of the line
    B. changing target markets
    C. disjointed corporate identification
    D. need for countering competitive strategies

11. The pricing strategy that allows customers to purchase services on an optional basis is called _____ pricing.

    A. scatter
    B. unbundled
    C. skimming
    D. penetration

12. If a company makes a line of similar products or has one dominant line, the _____ organizational system is probably most appropriate.

    A. product-planning committee
    B. marketing-manager
    C. new-product manager
    D. product manager

13. What type of market research tool is a list of bipolar adjective scales, using the scales either in place of or in addition to open questions?

    A. Multidimensional scaling
    B. Nonprobability sampling
    C. Semantic differential
    D. Disguised survey

14. The management of American Furniture calculated that an overall investment of $550,000 was necessary in a given year to yield net sales of $930,000. The company's net profit was $110,000. Before taxes, the company's return on investment was

    A. 12%   B. 20%   C. 32%   D. 59%

15. The MAIN advantage associated with market share analysis is

    A. ability to pinpoint coming trends
    B. enabling an aggressive or declining company to adjust its forecast and marketing efforts
    C. enabling experts to direct, interpret, and respond to concrete data
    D. concentrated focus on consumer attitudes

16. A company's traffic manager

    A. controls the level and allocation of merchandise throughout the year
    B. consolidates small shipments from many companies
    C. is responsible for storage and movement of goods within a company's warehouse facilities
    D. is in charge of physical distribution

17. Which of the following is NOT a typical difference between the marketing characteristics of services and the marketing of goods?

    A. Consumer choice is more difficult with services because of intangibility
    B. Impossibility of separating the producer from the product
    C. Focus on consumer attitudes and behaviors is narrowed to single consumers
    D. Prevention of storage, and increased risk, associated with perishability

18. Which of the following is an order-generating cost?

    A. Advertising
    B. Merchandise handling
    C. Filling out and handling orders
    D. Computer time

19. Which of the following is NOT considered to be an internal barrier to future growth in service industries?

    A. Little emphasis on research and development
    B. Limited competition
    C. Overspecialization of personnel
    D. Small size of the average service firm

20. A company conducts its sales analysis by starting with general market information and then computing a series of more specific market information. This approach is known as

    A. test marketing   B. market buildup method
    C. simple trend analysis   D. chain-ratio method

21. NOT generally considered to be one of the primary components of a physical distribution system is a

    A. set of inventories of goods
    B. wholesaler who will oversee and direct the physical transport of the inventories
    C. set of fixed facilities at which goods are produced or stored
    D. transportation network connecting the fixed facilities, as well as with customer receiving points

22. What is the term for the number of different product lines offered by a company?

    A. Width   B. Depth
    C. Scope   D. Consistency

23. For a wide variety of products, a small proportion of total consumers may account for a large percentage of a product or service's total sales. This market segmentation concept is known as the

    A. concentric integration
    B. heavy-half
    C. iceberg principle
    D. ideal point

24. Which of the following promotional activities offers the highest flexibility?

    A. Advertising
    B. Personal selling
    C. Publicity
    D. Sales promotions

25. The use of market research alone for marketing information collection involves certain risks. Which of the following is NOT one of these risks?

    A. Actions are more likely to be reactionary than anticipatory
    B. Time lags when new research study is involved
    C. Ineffective review of marketing plans and decisions
    D. Incomplete idea of consumer attitudes

KEY (CORRECT ANSWERS)

1.	C	11.	B
2.	B	12.	B
3.	C	13.	C
4.	D	14.	B
5.	A	15.	B
6.	C	16.	D
7.	C	17.	C
8.	A	18.	A
9.	B	19.	C
10.	A	20.	D

21.	B
22.	A
23.	B
24.	B
25.	D

EXAMINATION SECTION
TEST 1

DIRECTIONS: Each question or incomplete statement is followed by several suggested answers or completions. Select the one that BEST answers the question or completes the statement. *PRINT THE LETTER OF THE CORRECT ANSWER IN THE SPACE AT THE RIGHT.*

1. During the maturity period of a product's life cycle, a company's strategic marketing objective will generally be to

    A. improve competitive position
    B. maintain position
    C. accelerate market growth
    D. harvest

2. A franchiser can MOST effectively minimize the risks of product liability by

    A. carefully preparing the trademark licensing agreement
    B. using an agent or broker to determine distribution
    C. constructing a multi-channel distribution system
    D. avoiding entanglement in claims against licensees

3. Which of the following is not an advantage associated with product management organizations?

    A. Improved coordination of functional activities within and across product-market entries
    B. Long-term orientation on the part of product managers
    C. Ability to identify and react more quickly to threats and opportunities faced by individual product-market entries

4. The retailing of service products differs from that of physical goods in each of the following ways EXCEPT

    A. more difficult consumer choice
    B. tendency toward localization
    C. easier quality control
    D. heterogeneous delivery process

5. A _____ is a name, term, or symbol which is intended to identify the goods or services of one seller or group of sellers and to differentiate them from those of competitors.

    A. patent   B. brand
    C. copyright   D. trademark

6. According to the categories established by the VALS psychographic segments, the smallest psychographic segment of Americans is the _____ category.

    A. achievers   B. experiential
    C. integrated   D. societally conscious

7. _____ is NOT typically a characteristic of department store retailers.

   A. Large sales volume
   B. Wide product mix
   C. Self-service outlets
   D. Achieve most sales through apparel and cosmetics

8. Face-to-face selling is likely to be of great importance under each of the following conditions EXCEPT

   A. a small target market consisting of relatively few customers
   B. a technically complex product or service
   C. the use of an extensive distribution network
   D. a marketing strategy aimed at wresting market share away from established competitors

9. A company wants to target a market that is highly competitive, but the company's competitive position is estimated to be only moderate by marketing advisers. Typically, which of the following should be part of the company's strategy?

   A. Invest to grow at maximum digestible rate
   B. Invest to improve position only in areas where risk is low
   C. Reinforce vulnerable areas
   D. Defend strengths

10. Which of the following is not a major INTERNAL variable that affects a company's ability to implement particular marketing strategies?

    A. Fit between individual product marketing strategies and the company's higher-level corporate and business strategies
    B. Administrative relationships between strategic business units and other members of the distribution channel
    C. Mechanisms used to coordinate and resolve conflicts among departments
    D. Contents of the detailed marketing action plan for each product-market entry

11. Each of the following is a projective technique for analyzing consumers' motives EXCEPT

    A. depth interviews
    B. sentence completion tests
    C. balloon tests
    D. word-association tests

12. As a selling objective, the gathering of information is especially useful in the

    A. maturity phase of consumer durables
    B. marketing of most shopping goods
    C. shakeout period of specialty markets
    D. introductory or growth stage of industrial products

13. A new lower-priced brand of shampoo is introduced into a highly competitive market by a competitor with limited resources. Companies with strong existing brands are likely to respond in each of the following ways EXCEPT

A. hold prices the same
B. offer coupons, discounts, or larger sizes at the same price
C. lower prices dramatically to drive the competitors out
D. lower prices to the level of the new brand

14. When marketing managers attempt to control marketing activities, they frequently encounter several problems. Which of the following is NOT typically one of these problems?

    A. Information required to control marketing activities is unavailable
    B. Internal cost analysis is unavailable
    C. Frequent and unpredictable changes in environmental factors
    D. Time lag between marketing activities and their effects

15. Each of the following is a typical characteristic of one-level marketing channels EXCEPT

    A. retail sales personnel must often exert pressure on shoppers
    B. extensive postsale servicing demand
    C. usually involve companies with limited distribution allocation
    D. retail sales personnel must be more knowledgeable about the product

16. Which of the following is NOT a limitation associated with the use of profitability analysis as a means of organizational control?

    A. Many objectives can best be measured in non-financial terms.
    B. Costs associated with specific marketing activities need to be analyzed in different market segments and distribution channels.
    C. Profits can be affected by factors over which management has no control.
    D. Profit is a short-term measure and can be manipulated by actions that may prove dysfunctional in the longer term.

17. A market aggregation strategy is appropriate where the total market

    A. uses limited distribution channels
    B. has few differences in customer needs or desires
    C. is organizational in nature
    D. is concentrated in one particular geographic location

18. A company produces a food seasoning that is widely used in restaurants. If the company decides to introduce this seasoning into supermarkets for home use, it is likely that the

    A. company has discovered a new market segment
    B. product has experienced a decline in restaurant sales
    C. product has been slightly modified
    D. product line has been widened

19. Which of the following is NOT usually a type of organizational purchase?

    A. Discretionary purchase   B. Straight rebuy
    C. Modified rebuy   D. New-task purchase

20. In a growth market situation, a company defines its primary marketing objective as attracting a smaller share of new customers in a variety of smaller, specialized segments where customers' needs or preferences differ from those of early adopters in the mass market.
The company's marketing strategy could best be described as

   A. encirclement
   B. guerrilla attack
   C. leapfrog
   D. frontal attack

21. Contractual systems sponsored by wholesalers, which independent retailers can join, are known as

   A. manufacturer-sponsored franchises
   B. cooperative chains
   C. administered systems
   D. voluntary chains

22. The practice of skimming pricing is MOST likely to be used in the marketing of

   A. high-technology products
   B. clothing
   C. franchised restaurants
   D. low-margin household products

23. The institution with the authority to deal with trademark infringements is the

   A. Federal Trade Commission
   B. municipal, county, or state court
   C. Department of Commerce
   D. Patent and Trademark Office

24. In the relationship between a business unit and the company within which it operates, *centralization* refers to the

   A. location of decision authority and control within an organization's hierarchy
   B. degree to which decisions and working relationships are governed by formal rules and standard policies
   C. geographic location of the business unit in relation to the administrative center of the company
   D. division of tasks and activities across positions within the organizational unit

25. A leading stationery manufacturer, due to the large demand for its product, was able to force less desirable lines upon retailers, who had to accept these lines in order to receive the fast-moving items. Eventually, the manufacturer experienced an off-year, and the retailers struck back by refusing to take any items they did not want, even buying only minimal amounts of the faster-moving items. This situation is an example of

   A. trust-busting
   B. an administered system
   C. the natural retail cycle
   D. channel conflict

KEY (CORRECT ANSWERS)

1. B
2. A
3. C
4. C
5. B

6. C
7. C
8. A
9. C
10. B

11. A
12. D
13. C
14. B
15. C

16. B
17. B
18. A
19. A
20. A

21. D
22. A
23. B
24. A
25. D

TEST 2

DIRECTIONS: Each question or incomplete statement is followed by several suggested answers or completions. Select the one that BEST answers the question or completes the statement. *PRINT THE LETTER OF THE CORRECT ANSWER IN THE SPACE AT THE RIGHT.*

1. A company might decide to engage in the practice of penetration pricing in order to

    A. increase market share and gain greater visibility and market power
    B. create a high-quality image for the product
    C. clear out inventories of older models
    D. discourage potential competitors from entering the market at all

    1.____

2. When a buyer questions whether he or she should have purchased a product at all, or would have been better off purchasing another brand, this is an example of

    A. demarketing   B. cognitive dissonance
    C. consumerism   D. evoked set

    2.____

3. The primary responsibility of a company's sales force is to gain and maintain support for the company's products within the distribution channel by providing merchandising and promotional services to the channel members. The company's sales force is MOST likely composed of _____ sellers.

    A. new business   B. missionary
    C. technical   D. trade

    3.____

4. Under the Uniform Commercial Code, certain remedies are available to a party in a sales contract who claim a breach of the contract. The code sets forth each of the following specific measures for ascertaining the amount of damages to goods named in such a contract EXCEPT the _____ standard.

    A. resale   B. actual cash value
    C. market value   D. profit

    4.____

5. A company has adopted a prospector strategy for entrance into a certain market. Typically, a business unit in the company will perform best when one of its functional strengths is

    A. production   B. distribution
    C. financial management and control   D. marketing

    5.____

6. _____ is the specific term for the entity that permits . the identification of goods as the product of a particular maker, seller, or sponsor.

    A. patent   B. trademark
    C. copyright   D. brand

    6.____

7. A group of smaller hotel chains finds that they can make a reasonable profit by following the prices of the price leader – a large, nationwide chain as long as they can keep their hotels reasonably well-filled. To do this, the smaller chains advertise heavily and try to book as many meetings, conventions, and tours as possible.
This is an example of

    A. imitation   B. market saturation
    C. nonprice competition   D. leader pricing

    7.____

8. Which of the following consumer selections is likely to be most strongly influenced by a reference group?

   A. Radio
   B. Coffee
   C. Automobile
   D. Magazine or book

9. Generally, the practice of offering seasonal discounts to a consumer is beneficial in each of the following ways EXCEPT

   A. lower inventory carrying costs for the seller
   B. less overload on distribution facilities
   C. encourages buyer to pay as soon as possible
   D. less overtime pay for employees

10. The first introduction of a graphite golf club into the market was an example of

    A. adaptive replacement
    B. product innovation
    C. imitation
    D. line simplification

11. According to market research conventions, which of the following qualities or behaviors would be displayed by members of the lower-middle class?

    A. Tend to be brand loyal
    B. Buy relatively expensive homes to indicate social position
    C. Avoid mass merchandisers
    D. Common joint shopping of husband and wife

12. In a marketing audit, a company focuses on whether the company has adequate and timely information about consumers' satisfaction with its products. Which area of the company's marketing activities is being audited?

    A. Planning and control system
    B. Organization
    C. Objectives and strategy
    D. Marketing environment

13. A credit-card company decides to segment its market using a product-related approach. Most likely, the users will be segmented according to

    A. their level of disposable income
    B. the types of goods and services they use their cards for
    C. the frequency with which they use their cards
    D. the pattern of credit services they utilize

14. A personal characteristic considered to be important for missionary sellers is

    A. knowledge of customers
    B. maturity
    C. verbal skill
    D. empathy

15. Under the Uniform Commercial Code, the parties in a sales contract can conclude a contract for sale even if the price has not been settled. In such a case, the price will be considered to be a reasonable price at the time of delivery under any of the following conditions EXCEPT

    A. the price is to be fixed in good faith by the buyer or seller
    B. nothing at all has been said as to price
    C. the price is definitively scheduled for consideration by an impartial arbitrator
    D. the price is yet to be agreed upon by the parties and they fail to agree

16. A strategic business unit within a company desires a high level of autonomy within the organization. Which type of business strategy would be most conducive to this?

    A. Prospector
    B. Analyzer
    C. Differentiated defender
    D. Low-cost defender

17. In a certain marketing channel network, a wholesaler's markup on a certain product is 20%, and the retailer's markup is 50%. An end-use customer pays $300 for the product. What was the price at which the wholesaler purchased the product from the producer?

    A. $150   B. $166.67   C. $200   D. $233.34

18. Under the Uniform Commercial Code, certain remedies are available to a party in a sales contract who claim a breach of the contract. Generally, which of the following remedies is NOT available to the buyer in such a contract?

    A. Purchase of substitute goods, holding seller liable for any reasonable losses the buyer might have incurred in the cover operation
    B. Cancel the contract entirely, and recover moneys which might have been paid, as well as recovering damages
    C. Sue for possession of the goods
    D. Acceptance of nonconforming goods and suing for compensatory damages as well as punitive damages

19. A _____ is most likely to extend credit to customers.

    A. selling agent
    B. manufacturer's agent
    C. commission merchant
    D. broker

20. In exercising control over inventory, it is important to remember that individual reorders depend on

    A. the probability of obsolescence
    B. the trade-off between the cost of carrying larger inventories and the cost of processing small orders
    C. the total amount of capital tied up in inventory
    D. overall demand

21. The PRIMARY difference between a facilitating agency and a marketing channel member is that a facilitating agency

    A. does not perform negotiating functions
    B. is less specialized
    C. is not involved with physical distribution of a product
    D. has no influence over pricing

22. Most business firms judge their effectiveness in terms of

    A. total revenue
    B. profits as a percentage of sales
    C. segments controlled
    D. return on investment (ROI)

23. A market segmentation study describes a certain population as *typical light users* of the product under investigation. In this example, the study is using a _____ descriptor.

    A. customer needs
    B. person-related behavioral
    C. product-related behavioral
    D. demographic

24. Under which of the following conditions is a personal selling strategy targeted toward the development of new customers most appropriate?

    A. The product is in the introductory stage
    B. Business is pursuing a differentiated defender strategy
    C. Firm intentions to increase market share of a mature market
    D. Lengthy purchase decision process

25. Generally, the more conspicuous a product is, the more likely it is that a consumer's brand decision will be influenced by

    A. reference groups   B. family roles
    C. situational factors   D. demographics

KEY (CORRECT ANSWERS)

1.	D		11.	D
2.	B		12.	A
3.	D		13.	B
4.	B		14.	C
5.	D		15.	C
6.	B		16.	A
7.	C		17.	B
8.	C		18.	D
9.	C		19.	A
10.	A		20.	B

21. A
22. D
23. C
24. C
25. A

TEST 3

DIRECTIONS: Each question or incomplete statement is followed by several suggested answers or completions. Select the one that BEST answers the question or completes the statement. *PRINT THE LETTER OF THE CORRECT ANSWER IN THE SPACE AT THE RIGHT.*

1. Each of the following is a reason why marketing channels in a distribution system might change EXCEPT

    A. one or more middlemen find a way to increase their own profits or strength in the channel
    B. new technology
    C. one or more companies discover a less expensive way to distribute their goods
    D. greater customer service provisions offered by a company

    1.____

2. A blended *Scotch* whiskey, made in the United States, is priced at a low margin, and sells poorly. After the manufacturer raises the price of the product by $2 a bottle, without any change in the product or its packaging, sales increase dramatically.
This can be best explained by asserting that customers

    A. believe the product offers greater prestige
    B. mistakenly believe the product is a single-malt Scotch
    C. believe the quality of the product to be comparable to that of higher-priced whiskeys
    D. are more likely to believe the product was imported from Scotland

    2.____

3. A well-established personal computer manufacturer with several product lines introduces a new line of computers at a very low price, and receives an estimated $10 billion in orders before the machines are available at retail outlets. The introduction of this product line will most likely result in a *decrease* in the company's sales by

    A. discouraging competition that will supply long-term technological growth to the market
    B. starting a price war with competitors
    C. encouraging the proliferation of a horizontal marketing channel structure
    D. drawing customer attention away from other, higher-margin product lines

    3.____

4. In establishing physical distribution objectives, the distribution-center concept has a few distinct advantages. Which of the following is NOT one of these advantages?

    A. Greater control over shipments
    B. Justified expenditures on automated equipment for more efficient handling
    C. Lower total cost
    D. Goods can be shipped directly from producer in the form or number ordered by customers

    4.____

5. A company may want to use a salesforce compensation plan combining both salary and commission when

    A. company cannot closely control salesforce activities
    B. sales territories have relatively similar sales potentials
    C. when salespersons need to perform many non-selling activities
    D. highly aggressive selling is required

    5.____

6. Which of the following goods are characterized by limited availability, an emphasis on personal selling, and availability in a limited number of stores?

    A. Specialty
    B. Convenience
    C. Shopping
    D. Unsought

7. A company's pricing practice interacts with promotion expenditures in many ways. Which of the following statements is NOT true in the case of advertising for consumer products?

    A. Higher prices for a new type of consumer product can provide the funds necessary to advertise heavily, in order to inform people of the improved benefits offered by the new product.
    B. Advertising often has a greater effect on the sales of high-priced than low-priced products.
    C. Higher advertising expenditures can reduce the total cost of selling by preselling the buyer.
    D. Companies that want to support a high price for their product often spend a great deal on advertising.

8. When making purchase decisions, resellers typically consider each of the following factors EXCEPT

    A. amount of space required to handle a product
    B. lowest acceptable bid for products or services
    C. supplier's ability to provide adequate quantities when needed
    D. product demand

9. Generally, due to potential changes in cash flow and production practices, which department in a company would have the EASIEST time accepting a decision to simplify a product line?

    A. Higher-level management
    B. Sales
    C. Production
    D. Finance

10. In pinpointing the essential tasks of distribution, the producer must keep in mind the basic trade-relations mix. Which of the following is NOT an element of the trade-relations mix?

    A. Conditions of sale
    B. Price policy
    C. Trademark status
    D. Territorial rights

11. During the shakeout period of a product's life cycle, a company's investments in the product (R&D, working capital, and marketing) will generally be

    A. negative   B. low   C. moderate   D. high

12. A registered trademark can be made incontestable as soon as it has been in use, subsequent to the date of the certificate, for

    A. 6 months   B. 1 year   C. 5 years   D. 10 years

13. A large snack-food company periodically experiences declines in the sales of its products. In the long term, the company can probably BEST counteract the decrease in profits by

    A. spending more on promotion and advertising
    B. shifting its promotion and advertising to other market segments
    C. periodically introducing new product lines
    D. periodically changing the packaging of its products

14. According to the categories established by the VALS psychographic segments, most Americans fall into the category

    A. achievers   B. belongers
    C. societally conscious D. emulators

15. In a single year, company X sold $800,000 worth of its product. The entire industry sold a total of $9 million. What was the approximate market share of company X for this product in this year?

    A. .09%   B. 8.9%   C. 11.1%   D. 17.8%

16. Each of the following is a reason why a retailer might practice scrambled merchandising EXCEPT

    A. generation of more traffic
    B. generating brand loyalty
    C. increasing impulse purchases
    D. realizing higher profit margins

17. When a business faces an extremely complex and uncertain environment, which form of organization is MOST likely to be appropriate?

    A. Matrix   B. Product management
    C. Market management   D. Functional

18. The exemption of dedicated export-trade associations from existing antitrust legislation is the major provision of the_____ Act.

    A. Webb-Pomerene   B. Clayton
    C. Robinson-Patman   D. Federal Trade Commission

19. For a business that has adopted a differentiated defender strategy with respect to a certain market, which of the following policies would be LEAST appropriate?

    A. High salesforce expenditure as a percent of sales
    B. Relatively high prices
    C. Broad, technically sophisticated product lines
    D. Low trade promotion expenses as a percent of sales

20. Which of the following is categorized as a social influence on the consumer buying decision process?

    A. Personality   B. Reference group
    C. Attitude   D. Job status (promotion, firing, etc.)

21. A company's marketing department adopts the communication of product information as one of its primary selling objectives.
    Which of the following is LEAST likely to be true? The

    A. product is technically complex
    B. purchase decision is typically a lengthy process
    C. product is in the maturity stage of its life cycle
    D. purchase decision is influenced by multiple factors

22. In terms of trademark law, most foreign countries differ from the United States *primarily* in the

    A. means by which infringement is litigated
    B. legal definition of a trademark
    C. requirement of use as a prerequisite to registration
    D. distinction between a trademark and a service mark

23. Which of the following is an example of an indirect cost?

    A. Materials
    B. General management
    C. Advertising
    D. Labor

24. The tendency to remain loyal to a company rather than a particular brand or product is known as

    A. evoked set
    B. discrimination
    C. mental set
    D. generalization

25. The purpose of *push money* is to

    A. provide an incentive to retail sales personnel
    B. encourage transport agents to pay freight costs
    C. encourage customer trade-ins
    D. provide a buying incentive to customers

KEY (CORRECT ANSWERS)

1. D
2. C
3. D
4. D
5. B

6. C
7. B
8. B
9. A
10. C

11. C
12. C
13. C
14. B
15. B

16. B
17. A
18. A
19. C
20. B

21. C
22. C
23. B
24. D
25. A

TEST 4

DIRECTIONS: Each question or incomplete statement is followed by several suggested answers or completions. Select the one that BEST answers the question or completes the statement. *PRINT THE LETTER OF THE CORRECT ANSWER IN THE SPACE AT THE RIGHT.*

1. The total costs of producing an additional quantity of a product, less the total costs of producing the current quantity, will yield the _____ costs.

    A. total
    B. average total
    C. marginal
    D. total variable

2. Each of the following is a consideration associated with the profitability factor of a business analysis EXCEPT

    A. time to recoup initial costs
    B. risk
    C. control over price
    D. potential sales at different prices

3. A strategy in which one name is used for several products is known as _____ branding.

    A. family B. net C. line D. wide

4. Which of the following is NOT a common means of preventing or resolving channel conflict?

    A. Proper channel design
    B. Selective distribution
    C. Employment of cooperation techniques
    D. Exertion of power

5. Which of the following is a disadvantage associated with the sales force survey as a means of sales forecasting?

    A. Assumption that areas will behave similarly in the future
    B. Does not reveal traits of heavy users
    C. Lack of awareness of competitor's intentions
    D. Regions nor representative

6. Which of the following is typically controlled by a company's top management, rather than by the marketing department?

    A. Role of marketing decisions
    B. Selection of target markets
    C. Profit objectives
    D. Type of marketing organization

7. A disadvantage associated with independent ownership of a retail outlet is

    A. inflexibility
    B. much competition
    C. limited decision-making ability
    D. high investment costs

8. Advertising will dominate in a company's promotional mix when

   A. products are simple and inexpensive, and differential advantages are clear
   B. the market is small and concentrated, and organized consumers are involved
   C. customers expect assistance and service in retail stores
   D. the budget is limited or tailored to the needs of specific customers

9. Which of the following factors is NOT used to calculate the, target price of a product?

   A. Standard volume
   B. Variable per unit costs
   C. Investment costs
   D. Target ROI percentage

10. A manufacturer's brand

    A. is not widely advertised
    B. is targeted to price-conscious consumers
    C. has a price usually controlled by the dealer
    D. is usually part of a deep product line

11. Which of the following steps in a segmentation strategy would typically be performed FIRST?

    A. Establishing an appropriate marketing plan
    B. Selecting consumer segments
    C. Analyzing consumer similarities and differences
    D. Developing consumer group profiles

12. A company's retail merchandise manager

    A. supervises several buyers
    B. supervises the day-to-day activities of the store
    C. is responsible for purchasing items for resale
    D. is a buyer for a manufacturer, wholesaler, or retailer

13. Which of the following market research techniques would typically be best for discovering consumer attitudes?

    A. Simulation
    B. Survey
    C. Experimentation
    D. Observation

14. The MOST significant in number and volume of those engaged in the wholesaling business are

    A. merchant wholesalers
    B. assemblers
    C. manufacturer's sales branches
    D. merchandise agents and brokers

15. Which of the following types of organizational consumer decision processes involves the greatest amount of perceived risk?

    A. Impulse buy
    B. New task purchase
    C. Modified rebuy
    D. Straight rebuy

16. Each of the following is a consideration associated with the demand projection factor of a business analysis EXCEPT

    A. speed of consumer acceptance
    B. channel intensity
    C. per unit fixed costs
    D. seasonally of sales

17. Which of the following questions would appear on a disguised market research survey?

    A. At what time of day do you usually eat dinner?
    B. Which of the following is most important to you?
    C. What factors do you consider in the purchase of home furnishings?
    D. Are people who purchase sports cars status conscious;

18. Most franchisors require each of the following of a franchisee EXCEPT

    A. college education
    B. age 26-60
    C. owning one's own home
    D. able to finance leasehold improvements

19. A company conducts its sales analysis by gathering small, separate market segments and then aggregating them. This approach is known as

    A. consumer survey
    B. market buildup method
    C. simple trend analysis
    D. chain-ratio method

20. $\dfrac{\text{Cost of goods sold}}{\text{Net sales}}$ is a formula for which performance ratio?

    A. Stock turnover ratio
    B. Cost of goods sold ratio
    C. Return on investment
    D. Sales efficiency ratio

21. What is the term for the number of product items within each of the product lines offered by a company?

    A. Width   B. Depth   C. Scope   D. Consistency

22. In organizational purchasing for middlemen, the search for sources can have a large number of influences. Which of the following is NOT typically one of these influences?

    A. Past dates of sales for similar products
    B. Consumer surveys
    C. Shopping competitors' offerings
    D. Market research studies

23. What is the term for a form of price adjustment in which across-the-board price increases are published to supplement list prices?

    A. Bundling   B. Surcharge   C. Stimulus   D. Tariff

24. Which of the following promotional activities has the LOWEST overall cost per potential customer?

    A. Sales promotion
    B. Publicity
    C. Advertising
    D. Personal selling

25. In the multiple segmentation method for developing a target market,
    A. there is one product or service brand tailored to one consumer group
    B. there is a distinct price range for each consumer group
    C. a mass media promotion is used
    D. the object is a broad range of consumers

25.____

KEY (CORRECT ANSWERS)

1. C
2. D
3. A
4. B
5. C

6. A
7. B
8. A
9. B
10. D

11. C
12. A
13. B
14. A
15. B

16. C
17. D
18. A
19. B
20. B

21. B
22. B
23. B
24. C
25. B

EXAMINATION SECTION
TEST 1

DIRECTIONS: Each question or incomplete statement is followed by several suggested answers or completions. Select the one that BEST answers the question or completes the statement. *PRINT THE LETTER OF THE CORRECT ANSWER IN THE SPACE AT THE RIGHT.*

1. The interest rate that the Federal Reserve charges for loans to its member banks is called the _____ rate. 1.____

    A. secured
    B. open-market
    C. discount
    D. prime

2. The narrowest commonly used measure of money is 2.____

    A. currency, demand deposits, and time deposits
    B. bills and coin
    C. M1
    D. M2

3. Which of the following is NOT an element of the theory of asset demand? The quantity demanded of an asset is 3.____

    A. positively related to the risk of its return relative to alternative assets
    B. usually positively related to wealth, with the response being greater if the asset is a luxury rather than a necessity
    C. positively related to its expected return relative to alternative assets
    D. positively related to its liquidity relative to alternative assets

4. The face value of a bond is referred to as its 4.____

    A. denomination
    B. equity value
    C. market value
    D. share value

5. The real purpose of requiring a *compensating balance* in a loan contract is to 5.____

    A. implement a floating rate
    B. compensate the bank for loan service rendered
    C. force collateral in the form of reserves
    D. serve as an indirect means of increasing the bank's return on a loan

6. A book of original entry is referred to as the 6.____

    A. general journal
    B. income statement
    C. source document
    D. general ledger

7. What is the term for a perpetual bond with no maturity date and no repayment of principal that periodically makes fixed coupon payments? 7.____

    A. Consol   B. Fiat   C. Call   D. Hedge

8. The Federal Reserve typically encourages banks to make loans by 8.____

    A. raising the Federal Reserve funds rate
    B. raising the prime interest rate

C. lowering margin requirements
D. lowering the discount rate

9. A 20-year bond is purchased for $1000. Its initial yield to maturity is 10%, and the yield to maturity next year will be 20%. The ultimate rate of return for the bond will be

   A. -38.4%   B. -15.9%   C. +1.7%   D. +10.0%

10. When reserve requirements are low, there is

    A. a reduction in the overall money supply
    B. less money to lend to customers
    C. an economic slowdown
    D. an increase in the overall money supply

11. _____ law specifies the maximum interest rate that borrowers may be charged on specific types of loans.

    A. Civil   B. Usury   C. Finance   D. Lending

12. What is the term for a commercial draft that is payable whenever the drawer wishes?

    A. Sight draft   B. Debenture
    C. Convertible invoice   D. Time draft

13. At a Federal funds rate of 12% per annum, lending $500,000 will bring in _____ daily.

    A. $60.00   B. $81.77   C. $164.38   D. $416.66

14. Which of the following is the immediate source of a bank's financial statement?

    A. Trial balance   B. Checkbook
    C. Journal   D. Ledger

15. When a bank maintains a deposit with another bank, the depositing bank is known as the

    A. correspondent   B. twister
    C. guarantor   D. respondent

16. Which of the following best describes what happened in the banking industry during the 1980s?

    A. Banks became more willing to make commercial loans.
    B. An increasing number of banks failed.
    C. Bank profits rose steadily.
    D. The number of banks increased dramatically.

17. The cost of indirect finance is often lower than that of direct finance for each of the following reasons EXCEPT

    A. maturity transformation   B. information costs
    C. reserve requirements   D. diversification

18. Amounts that are on deposit in checking accounts are described as

    A. near-monies   B. demand deposits
    C. transfer deposits D. time deposits

19. Faced with the question of whether to buy and hold an asset or whether to buy one asset rather than another, an individual will typically consider each of the following factors EXCEPT

    A. expected return
    B. liquidity
    C. risk
    D. reserve requirements

    19.____

20. Which of the following are NOT an element of the income statement?

    A. Liabilities
    B. Operating expenses
    C. Net income or loss
    D. Revenues

    20.____

21. Under a traditional approach, which of the following would NOT be included in *primary* reserves?

    A. Interbank deposits
    B. Vault cash
    C. CDs
    D. Excess reserves

    21.____

22. Of the following, which are liquidity measures?

    A. Cash flow and return on investment
    B. Earnings per share and net profit margin
    C. Accounts receivable and notes receivable
    D. Quick ratio and current ratio

    22.____

23. In addition to complying with regulatory mandates, a bank's primary reserves serve to

    A. provide long-term liquidity
    B. provide investment opportunities
    C. provide a cushion against defaults
    D. meet the institution's immediate needs

    23.____

24. Activity ratios are used to determine

    A. a bank's profitability
    B. its ability to pay its short-term debts
    C. how well it manages its assets
    D. its ability to pay its long-term debts

    24.____

25. Among contractual savings institutions, which of the following currently account for the greatest total asset value?

    A. Private pension funds
    B. State and local government retirement funds
    C. Fire and casualty insurance companies
    D. Life insurance companies

    25.____

KEY (CORRECT ANSWERS)

1.	C	11.	B
2.	C	12.	A
3.	A	13.	C
4.	A	14.	A
5.	D	15.	D
6.	A	16.	B
7.	A	17.	C
8.	B	18.	B
9.	A	19.	D
10.	D	20.	A

21. C
22. D
23. D
24. C
25. A

TEST 2

DIRECTIONS: Each question or incomplete statement is followed by several suggested answers or completions. Select the one that BEST answers the question or completes the statement. *PRINT THE LETTER OF THE CORRECT ANSWER IN THE SPACE AT THE RIGHT.*

1. *Short-term* loans are usually paid within a term of _____ year(s). 1.____

   A. one B. three C. five D. ten

2. The liability theory of bank management originally found its strongest advocates in 2.____

   A. credit unions
   B. state banks
   C. limited-service banks
   D. large money market banks

3. When changed by the Federal Reserve, the discount rate is MOST likely to influence the 3.____

   A. margin requirements B. stock market gains
   C. reserve requirements D. prime interest rate

4. Banks tend to prefer government debt in their investments for each of the following reasons EXCEPT 4.____

   A. legal constraints B. liquidity
   C. rate of return D. income

5. _____ analysis is the term for the comparison of two elements from the same year's financial data. 5.____

   A. Regression B. Trend
   C. Statistical D. Ratio

6. The L measure of money adds each of the following to the M-3 measure EXCEPT 6.____

   A. money market mutual fund shares
   B. savings bonds
   C. banker's acceptances
   D. commercial paper

7. A firm has assets of $1,000,000 and liabilities of $400,000. The firm's net worth must be 7.____

   A. $1,400,000 B. $1,000,000
   C. $600,000 D. $200,000

8. What is the term for the process of transferring information from a general journal to a general ledger? 8.____

   A. Recording B. Posting
   C. Journalizing D. Transposition

163

9. A $1000 bond matures in two years, and pays a coupon rate of 10%. Assume that yields in the present market equal 15%. How much is the bond worth today?

   A. $864.64   B. $918.71   C. $1100   D. $1150

10. The _____ rate is the rate which banks charge each other for overnight loans.

    A. Federal Reserve funds
    B. prime interest
    C. discount
    D. reserve

11. If a bank finds that it has too high an equity multiplier and is short on bank capital, it may typically deal with this problem in one of each of the following ways EXCEPT

    A. raising capital by issuing equity
    B. keeping capital at the same level, but reducing the amount of its assets by making fewer loans or selling off securities
    C. keeping capital at the same level, but reducing its liabilities with the use of excess reserves
    D. raising capital by reducing its dividends to shareholders

12. Accrued expenses, accounts payable, and notes payable are all examples of

    A. current assets
    B. long-term liabilities
    C. equity
    D. current liabilities

13. Other than corporate stocks, which money market debt instrument currently accounts for the greatest proportion of amounts outstanding?

    A. Residential mortgages
    B. State and local government bonds
    C. Corporate bonds
    D. U.S. government securities

14. If it wishes to slow the economy, the Federal Reserve is likely to

    A. increase the discount rate
    B. sell government securities
    C. increase reserve requirements
    D. lower the prime rate

15. The theory of bank management that rests on the fact that a bank's liquidity is influenced by the maturity pattern of loans is called the _____ theory.

    A. commercial loan
    B. anticipated-income
    C. asset-allocation
    D. shiftability

16. The Federal Reserve has four basic tools at its disposal for regulating the money supply and expanding the economy.
    Which of the following is NOT one of these?
    It may

    A. engage in closed-market operations
    B. set the terms of credit for certain types of loans
    C. change the discount rate
    D. change reserve requirements

17. _____ analysis is the method for measuring interest-rate risk which examines the sensitivity of the market value of a bank's total assets and liabilities to changes in interest rates.

    A. Basis point
    B. Gap
    C. Mean reversion
    D. Duration

18. What is to be determined by the use of liquidity measures in accounting?

    A. Ability to pay short-term debts
    B. Management of assets
    C. Profitability
    D. Ability to pay long-term debts

19. A depositer takes a deposit check to her bank and decides not to deposit the entire sum, but rather to take out some cash instead. This is an example of _____ leakage.

    A. excess reserve
    B. borrowed reserve
    C. time deposit
    D. cash

20. Each of the following is a commonly used profitability ratio EXCEPT

    A. earnings per share
    B. current ratio
    C. return on investment
    D. net profit margin

21. Which of the following is a measure of the sensitivity of an asset's return to changes in the value of a market portfolio?

    A. Cost-push inflation
    B. Beta
    C. Load
    D. Quota

22. The representative for bond owners is referred to as the

    A. trustee
    B. attorney
    C. agent
    D. broker

23. What member of the banking community accepts deposits and uses those deposits to make loans for profit?

    A. Limited-service bank
    B. Credit union
    C. Thrift institution
    D. Commercial bank

24. Which of the following credit-market instruments is bought at a price below its face value?

    A. Zero-coupon bond
    B. Fixed-payment loan
    C. Coupon bond
    D. Simple loan

25. Which of the following was NOT a function of the Federal Deposit Insurance Corporation Improvement Act (FDICIA) of 1991?
    The

    A. limitation of brokered deposits
    B. raising of deposit insurance premiums
    C. increase of capital requirements and reporting requirements
    D. recapitalization of the FDIC

KEY (CORRECT ANSWERS)

1. A
2. D
3. D
4. C
5. D
6. A
7. C
8. B
9. B
10. A
11. C
12. D
13. A
14. C
15. B
16. A
17. D
18. A
19. D
20. B
21. B
22. A
23. C
24. A
25. B

EXAMINATION SECTION
TEST 1

DIRECTIONS: Each question or incomplete statement is followed by several suggested answers or completions. Select the one that BEST answers the question or completes the statement. *PRINT THE LETTER OF THE CORRECT ANSWER IN THE SPACE AT THE RIGHT.*

1. In the preparation of a balance sheet, failure to consider the inventory of office supplies will result in _____ assets and _____.

    A. overstating; overstating liabilities
    B. understating; overstating capital
    C. understating; understating capital
    D. overstating; understating liabilities

2. The annual federal unemployment tax is paid by the

    A. employer *only*
    B. employee *only*
    C. employer and the employee equally
    D. employee, up to a maximum of 30 cents per week, and the balance is paid by the employer

3. Which are NORMALLY considered as current assets?

    A. Bank overdrafts
    B. Prepaid expenses
    C. Accrued expenses
    D. Payroll taxes

4. What type of ledger account is a summary of a number of accounts in another ledger? The _____ account.

    A. controlling
    B. subsidiary
    C. asset
    D. proprietorship

5. The PRIMARY purpose of a petty cash fund is to

    A. provide a fund for paying all miscellaneous expenses
    B. take the place of the cash account
    C. provide a common drawing fund for the owners of the business
    D. avoid entering a number of small amounts in the Cash Payments Journal

6. In the absence of a written agreement, profits in a partnership would be divided

    A. in proportion to the investment of the partners
    B. on an equitable basis depending on the time and effort spent by the partners
    C. equally
    D. on a ratio of investment basis, giving the senior partner preference

7. Which account represents a subtraction or decrease to an income account?

    A. Purchase Returns & Allowances
    B. Sales Returns & Allowances
    C. Freight In
    D. Prepaid Rent

8. If the Interest Expense account showed a debit balance of $210 as of December 31, and $40 of this amount was prepaid on Notes Payable, which statement is CORRECT as of December 31?

   A. Prepaid Interest of $170 should be shown as a deferred expense in the balance sheet.
   B. Interest Expense should be shown in the Income Statement as $210.
   C. Prepaid Interest of $40 should be listed as a deferred credit to income in the balance sheet.
   D. Interest Expense should be shown in the Income Statement as $170.

9. When prices are rising, which inventory-valuation method results in the LOWEST inventory value?

   A. FIFO
   B. LIFO
   C. Average cost
   D. Declining balance

10. Which of the following is a CORRECT procedure in preparing a bank reconciliation?

    A. Deposits in transit should be added to the cash balance on the books, and outstanding checks should be deducted from the cash balance on the bank statement.
    B. The cash balance on the bank statement and the cash balance on the books should be equal if there are deposits in transit and outstanding checks.
    C. Outstanding checks should be deducted from the cash balance on the books.
    D. Any service charge should be deducted from the check stub balance.

11. Which ratio indicates that there may NOT be enough on hand to meet current obligations?

    A. $\dfrac{\text{fixed assets}}{\text{fixed liabilities}} = \dfrac{2}{3}$
    B. $\dfrac{\text{total assets}}{\text{total obligations}} = \dfrac{3}{5}$
    C. $\dfrac{\text{current assets}}{\text{current liabilities}} = \dfrac{1}{3}$
    D. $\dfrac{\text{current assets}}{\text{fixed liabilities}} = \dfrac{1}{2}$

12. Which asset is NOT subject to depreciation?

    A. Factory equipment
    B. Land
    C. Buildings
    D. Machinery

13. Which form is prepared to verify that the total of the account balances in the Customers Ledger agrees with the balance in the controlling account in the General Ledger?

    A. Worksheet
    B. Schedule of accounts payable
    C. Schedule of accounts receivable
    D. Trial balance

14. If the merchandise inventory on hand at the end of the year was overstated, what will be the result of this error? 14.____

    A. *Understatement* of income for the year
    B. *Overstatement* of income for the year
    C. *Understatement* of assets at the end of the year
    D. No effect on income or assets

15. Working capital is found by subtracting the total current liabilities from the total 15.____

    A. fixed liabilities   B. fixed assets
    C. current income   D. current assets

16. Which is the CORRECT procedure for calculating the rate of merchandise turnover? 16.____

    A. Gross Sales divided by Net Sales
    B. Cost of Sales divided by Average Inventory
    C. Net Purchases divided by Average Inventory
    D. Gross Purchases divided by Net Purchases

17. The books of the Atlas Cement Corporation show a net profit of $142,000. To close the Profit and Loss account of the corporation at the end of the year, the account CREDITED should be 17.____

    A. Earned Surplus   B. Capital Stock
    C. C. Atlas, Capital   D. C. Atlas, Personal

18. The bank statement at the end of the month indicated a bank charge for printing a new checkbook. 18.____
    How is this information recorded?
    Debit

    A. Cash and credit Office Supplies
    B. Office Supplies and credit the Bank Charges
    C. the Bank Charges and credit Office Supplies
    D. Miscellaneous Expense and credit Cash

19. The Allowance for Doubtful Accounts appears on the balance sheet as a deduction from 19.____

    A. Accounts Receivable   B. Notes Receivable
    C. Accounts Payable   D. Notes Payable

20. The Tucker Equipment Corporation had a $45,000 profit for the year ended December 31. 20.____
    Which would be the PROPER entry to close the Income and Expense account at the end of the year?
    Debit Income and Expense Summary; credit

    A. Tucker, Capital   B. Tucker, Drawing
    C. Retained Earnings   D. Capital Stock

21. A failure to record a purchases invoice would be discovered when the   21.____

    A. monthly statement of account is sent to the customer
    B. check is received from the customer
    C. check is sent to the creditor
    D. statement of account is received from the creditor

22. Which General Ledger account would appear in a post-closing trial balance?   22.____

    A. Notes Receivable   B. Bad Debts Expense
    C. Sales Discount   D. Fee Income

23. Which deduction is affected by the number of exemptions claimed?   23.____

    A. State Disability   B. State income tax
    C. FICA tax   D. Workers' Compensation

24. The face value of a 60-day, 12% promissory note is $900.   24.____
    The maturity value of this note will be

    A. $909   B. $900   C. $918   D. $1,008

25. An invoice dated March 10, terms 2/10, n/30, should be paid no later than   25.____

    A. March 20   B. March 31   C. April 9   D. April 10

KEY (CORRECT ANSWERS)

1. C   11. C
2. A   12. B
3. B   13. C
4. A   14. B
5. D   15. D

6. C   16. B
7. B   17. A
8. D   18. D
9. B   19. A
10. D   20. C

21. D
22. A
23. B
24. C
25. C

TEST 2

DIRECTIONS: Each question or incomplete statement is followed by several suggested answers or completions. Select the one that BEST answers the question or completes the statement. *PRINT THE LETTER OF THE CORRECT ANSWER IN THE SPACE AT THE RIGHT.*

1. Which is NOT an essential element of a computer system? 1.____

    A. Input
    B. Central processing unit
    C. Verifier
    D. Output

2. The general ledger account that would NOT appear in a post-closing trial balance would be 2.____

    A. Cash
    B. Accounts Payable
    C. Furniture and Fixtures
    D. Sales Income

3. Ralph Hanley, age 45, supports his wife and three children. Mr. Hanley is the only member of the family required to file an income tax return. What is the MAXIMUM number of exemptions he can claim? 3.____

    A. One   B. Five   C. Three   D. Four

4. The cost of a fixed asset minus the allowance for depreciation (accumulated depreciation) is the _____ value. 4.____

    A. market   B. cost   C. liquidation   D. book

5. The form used by a bookkeeper in summarizing adjustments and information which will be used in preparing statements is called a 5.____

    A. journal
    B. balance sheet
    C. ledger
    D. worksheet

6. When a large number of transactions of a particular kind are to be entered in bookkeeping records, it is USUALLY advisable to use 6.____

    A. cash records
    B. controlling accounts
    C. special journals
    D. special ledgers

7. The petty cash book shows a petty cash balance of $9.80 on May 31. The petty cash box contains only $9.10.
What account will be debited to record the $.70 difference? 7.____

    A. Cash
    B. Petty Cash
    C. Cash Short and Over
    D. Petty Cash Expense

8. The ONLY difference between the books of a partnership and those of a sole proprietorship appears in the _____ accounts. 8.____

    A. proprietorship
    B. liability
    C. asset
    D. expense

9. The earnings of a corporation are FIRST recorded as a credit to an account called 9.____

    A. Dividends Payable
    B. Capital Stock Authorized
    C. Retained Earnings
    D. Profit and Loss Summary

171

10. A firm purchased a new delivery truck for $2,900 and sold it four years later for $500. The Allowance for Depreciation of Delivery Equipment account was credited for $580 at the end of each of the four years.
    When the machine was sold, there was a

    A. loss of $80
    B. loss of $1,820
    C. loss of $2,400
    D. gain of $80

11. FICA taxes are paid by

    A. employees *only*
    B. employers *only*
    C. both employees and employers
    D. neither employees nor employers

12. Which phase of the data processing cycle is the SAME as calculating net pay in a manual system?

    A. Input   B. Processing   C. Storing   D. Output

13. Which error will cause the trial balance to be out of balance?

    A. A sales invoice for $60 was entered in the Sales Journal for $600.
    B. A credit to office furniture in the journal was posted as a credit to office machines in the ledger.
    C. A debit to advertising expense in the journal was posted as a debit to miscellaneous expense in the ledger.
    D. A debit to office equipment in the journal was posted as a credit to office equipment in the ledger.

14. The collection of a bad debt previously written off will result in a(n)

    A. *decrease* in assets
    B. *decrease* in capital
    C. *increase* in assets
    D. *increase* in liabilities

15. Which account does NOT belong in the group?

    A. Notes Receivable
    B. Building
    C. Office Equipment
    D. Delivery Truck

16. The adjusting entry to record the estimated bad debts is debit _____ and credit _____.

    A. Allowance for Bad Debts; Bad Debts Expense
    B. Bad Debts Expense; Allowance for Bad Debts
    C. Allowance for Bad Debts; Accounts Receivable
    D. Bad Debts Expense; Accounts Receivable

17. At the end of the year, which account should be closed into the income and expense summary?

    A. Freight In
    B. Allowance for Doubtful Accounts
    C. Notes Receivable
    D. Petty Cash

18. Which form is prepared to aid in verifying that the customer's account balances in the customer's ledger agree with the balance in the Accounts Receivable account in the general ledger?

    A. Worksheet
    B. Schedule of Accounts Payable
    C. Schedule of Accounts Receivable
    D. Trial Balance

19. In the preparation of an income statement, failure to consider accrued wages will result in

    A. *overstating* operating expense and understating net profit
    B. *overstating* net profit *only*
    C. *understating* operating expense and overstating net profit
    D. *understating* operating expense *only*

20. The CORRECT formula for determining the rate of merchandise turnover is

    A. cost of goods sold divided by average inventory
    B. net sales divided by net purchases
    C. gross sales divided by ending inventory
    D. average inventory divided by cost of goods sold

21. A legal characteristic of a corporation is _____ liability.

    A. contingent   B. limited
    C. unlimited   D. deferred

22. A customer's check you had deposited is returned to you by the bank labeled *Dishonored*.
    What entries would be made as a result of this action? Debit _____ and credit _____.

    A. cash; customer's account
    B. miscellaneous expense; cash
    C. customer's account; capital
    D. customer's account; cash

23. The TOTAL capital of a corporation may be found by adding

    A. assets and liabilities
    B. assets and capital stock
    C. liabilities and capital stock
    D. earned surplus and capital stock

24. The source of an entry made in the Petty Cash book is the

    A. general ledger   B. voucher
    C. register   D. general journal

25. Which account is debited to record interest earned but not yet due?

    A. Deferred Interest
    B. Interest Receivable
    C. Interest Income
    D. Income and Expense Summary

KEY (CORRECT ANSWERS)

1. C
2. D
3. B
4. D
5. D
6. C
7. C
8. A
9. C
10. A

11. C
12. B
13. D
14. C
15. A
16. B
17. A
18. C
19. C
20. A

21. B
22. D
23. D
24. B
25. B

TEST 3

DIRECTIONS: Each question or incomplete statement is followed by several suggested answers or completions. Select the one that BEST answers the question or completes the statement. *PRINT THE LETTER OF THE CORRECT ANSWER IN THE SPACE AT THE RIGHT.*

1. Which reason should NOT generally be used by an employer when making a hiring decision?
   An applicant('s)

   A. resume reveals a lack of job-related skills
   B. attendance record on a previous job is poor
   C. has improperly prepared the job application
   D. is married

   1.____

2. Graves, Owens, and Smith formed a partnership and invested $15,000 each. If the firm made a profit of $18,000 last year and profits and losses were shared equally, what was Owens' share of the net profit?

   A. $1,000 B. $5,000 C. $6,000 D. $9,000

   2.____

3. The bank statement balance of the Bedford Co. on May 31 was $3,263.28. The checkbook balance was $3,119.06. A reconciliation showed that the outstanding checks totaled $147.22 and that there was a bank service charge of $3.00. The CORRECT checkbook balance should be

   A. $3,260.28 B. $3,122.06 C. $3,116.06 D. $3,266.28

   3.____

4. Which account is shown in a post-closing trial balance?

   A. Prepaid Insurance   B. Fees Income
   C. Purchases   D. Freight In

   4.____

5. A check endorsed *For deposit only (signed) Samuel Jones* is an example of a _____ endorsement.

   A. full B. blank C. complete D. restrictive

   5.____

6. The selling price of a share of stock as published in a daily newspaper is called the _____ value.

   A. book B. face C. par D. market

   6.____

7. Which is obtained by dividing the cost of goods sold by the average inventory?

   A. Current ratio
   B. Merchandise inventory turnover
   C. Average rate of mark-up
   D. Acid-test ratio

   7.____

8. A Suzuki truck costing $39,000 is expected to have a useful life of six years and a salvage value of $3,000.
   If $6,000 is debited to the depreciation expense account each year for six years, what method of depreciation is used?

   A. Units of production   B. Straight line
   C. Declining balance   D. Sum of the years digits

   8.____

175

9. Which form is prepared to aid in verifying that the customer's account balances in the customer's ledger agree with the balance in the Accounts Receivable account in the General Ledger?

   A. Worksheet
   B. Schedule of Accounts Payable
   C. Schedule of Accounts Receivable
   D. Trial Balance

10. In the preparation of a balance sheet, failure to consider commissions owed to salespersons will result in _____ liabilities and _____ capital.

    A. understating; overstating
    B. understating; understating
    C. overstating; overstating
    D. overstating; understating

11. A financial statement generated by a computer is an example of a(n)

    A. audit trail
    B. output
    C. input
    D. program

12. Merchandise was sold for $150 cash plus a 3% sales tax. The CORRECT credit(s) should be

    A. Sales Income $150, Sales Taxes Payable $4.50
    B. Sales Income $154.50
    C. Merchandise $150, Sales Taxes Payable $4.50
    D. Sales Income $150

13. The bookkeeper should prepare a bank reconciliation MAINLY to determine

    A. which checks are outstanding
    B. whether the checkbook balance and the bank statement balance are in agreement
    C. the total amount of checks written during the month
    D. the total amount of cash deposited during the month

14. Which is the CORRECT procedure for calculating the rate of merchandise turnover?

    A. Gross Sales divided by Net Sales
    B. Cost of Goods Sold divided by Average Inventory
    C. Net Purchases divided by Average Inventory
    D. Gross Purchases divided by Net Purchases

15. Which previous job should be listed FIRST on a job application form? The

    A. least recent job
    B. most recent job
    C. job you liked best
    D. job which paid the most

16. Failure to record cash sales will result in

    A. *overstatement* of profit
    B. *understatement* of profit
    C. *understatement* of liabilities
    D. *overstatement* of capital

17. When a fixed asset is repaired, the cost of the repairs should be _____ account.   17.____

    A. *debited* to the asset
    B. *debited* to the expense
    C. *credited* to the proprietor's capital
    D. *credited* to the asset

18. The form used by a bookkeeper to summarize information which will be used in preparing financial statements is called a   18.____

    A. journal   B. balance sheet
    C. ledger   D. worksheet

19. Which type of ledger account is a summary of a number of accounts in another ledger? _____ account.   19.____

    A. Controlling   B. Subsidiary
    C. Asset   D. Proprietorship

20. What is the summary entry on the Purchases Journal?
    Debit _____ and credit _____.   20.____

    A. Accounts Payable; Merchandise Purchases
    B. Accounts Receivable; Merchandise Purchases
    C. Merchandise Purchases; Accounts Receivable
    D. Merchandise Purchases; Accounts Payable

21. The source document for entries made in the Sales Journal is a(n)   21.____

    A. credit memo   B. statement of accounts
    C. invoice   D. bill of lading

22. A Trial Balance which is in balance would NOT reveal the   22.____

    A. omission of the credit part of an entry
    B. posting of the same debit twice
    C. omission of an entire transaction
    D. omission of an account with a balance

23. A financial statement prepared by a computerized accounting system is an example of   23.____

    A. input   B. output
    C. flowcharting   D. programming

24. The form which the payroll clerk gives to each employee to show gross earnings and taxes withheld for the year is a   24.____

    A. W-2   B. W-3   C. W-4   D. 1040

25. Who would be the LEAST appropriate reference on an application for a job? A   25.____

    A. relative
    B. guidance counselor
    C. former employer
    D. prominent member of the community

KEY (CORRECT ANSWERS)

1. D
2. C
3. C
4. A
5. D

6. D
7. B
8. B
9. C
10. A

11. B
12. A
13. B
14. B
15. B

16. B
17. B
18. D
19. A
20. D

21. C
22. C
23. B
24. A
25. A

www.ingramcontent.com/pod-product-compliance
Lightning Source LLC
Chambersburg PA
CBHW082038300426
44117CB00015B/2523